Lower floor

Key

🚹 Toilets	🍽 Great Court R	
♿ Accessible toilet	☕ Café	🎧 Audio guide
🚼 Baby changing	*i* Information	🪜 Stairs
🍼 Baby feeding	🎟 Tickets & Membership	Lift
🧺 Shop	**F** Families Desk (weekends and school holidays only)	Level access lift

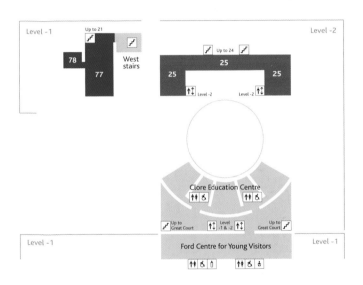

*Ask at the Information Desk in the Great Court for opening times of Rooms 16, 20a, 33a, 77 and 78.

Please note that some galleries may be closed at short notice due to unforseen circumstances or refurbishment.

■ Africa
Africa
The Sainsbury Galleries
   Room 25

■ Ancient Greece and Rome
Greek and Roman
   architecture
   Room 77 *
Classical inscriptions
   Room 78 *

The Clore Centre for Education
Hugh and Catherine Stevenson Lecture Theatre
Claus Moser Room
BP Lecture Theatre
Studio
Raymond and Beverly Sackler Rooms
Samsung Digital Discovery Centre

Ford Centre for Young Visitors

First published in 2016 by the British Museum
Great Russell Street
London WC1B 3DG

ISBN 9780714151069
Reprinted 2017

Illustrations in this publication appear by kind permission of the following:
p. 13 *Tree of Life* © Kester
p. 15 *Throne of Weapons* © Kester
p. 15 *Man's Cloth* © El Anatsui
p. 71 *Samramansang Moon Jar #1* © Reproduced by permission of the artist
p. 105 Glazed brick panel showing a lion © Staatliche Museen zu Berlin –
    Vorderasiatisches Museum, photograph Olaf M. Tessmer
p. 112 *The Rosetta Vase* © Reproduced by permission of the artist
p. 117 *The Atomic Apocalypse* © The Linares family
p. 123 *Stately plump Buck Milligan* © Estate of the artist

A catalogue record for this book is available from the British Library
Photography by the British Museum Department of Photography and Imaging
Printed and bound in Italy by Printer Trento
Designed by Zach John Design

Contents

Map

Introduction to the British Museum   4

The Great Court   6

Visitor information   9

Africa   12

Americas   18

Ancient Egypt   24

Ancient Greece and Rome   36

Asia   64

Europe   78

Middle East   92

Themes

    Enlightenment   110

    Collecting the world   112

    The Waddesdon Bequest   114

    Living and Dying   116

    Clocks and watches   118

    Money   120

    Prints and drawings   122

List of objects   126

Introduction to the British Museum

Physician and collector Sir Hans Sloane bequeathed his collection of over 71,000 objects from around the world to the nation in his will. On his death in 1753 it became the founding collection of the British Museum, the first national public museum in the world. It was first housed in Montagu House, a 17th-century mansion on the site of today's building. From the beginning it granted free admission to all 'studious and curious persons'.

Sloane's original collection included antiquities, coins and medals, natural history specimens and a large library. The natural history collection moved to South Kensington in the 1880s, and the library collection was relocated in 1997. The Museum's holdings now comprise over eight million objects spanning the history of the world's cultures, from the stone tools of early humans to 21st-century prints.

The British Museum is a vast place, with over seventy galleries and a huge range of extraordinary objects. This guide will help you plan your visit and find your way to the galleries and objects that you would like to see.

The Great Court

Like the collection, the Museum building has expanded over time. The four main wings, which form the core of today's building, were designed in 1823. The domed Reading Room at the heart of the Museum was completed in 1857 and originally housed the Museum's library. It was hailed as one of the great sights of London and became a world-famous centre of learning with famous readers including Bram Stoker, Sir Arthur Conan Doyle and even Lenin.

The Reading Room is now enclosed by the Great Court, which was added in 2000. Lord Norman Foster designed the space, which transformed the Museum's inner courtyard into the largest covered public square in Europe.

Visitor information

Galleries are open daily 10.00–17.30, until 20.30 on Fridays. Please note that galleries start closing 10 minutes before the published closing times.

The cloakroom is located to the west of the Main entrance (£).

Sketching with pencil in the galleries is allowed and photography is permitted in selected galleries for non-commercial uses.

To help everyone enjoy the Museum, please:

• keep phones on silent and don't take calls in galleries

• don't touch the objects

• don't smoke on the premises

• don't eat or drink in the galleries

If you have any questions, ask at the Information Desk in the Great Court. There are numerous events and talks in the Museum every day. Information about these can be found on the digital screens in the Great Court and from the Information Desk.

Exhibitions

Make the most of your visit

Special temporary exhibitions

See world-class exhibitions in our stunning exhibitions galleries. These unique displays feature treasures from the Museum's collection presented in new and exciting ways alongside spectacular loans.
Tickets are available from the Ticket Desk in the Great Court. Under 16s go free to all exhibitions. Inside each exhibition you'll find family guides and activities to explore more together.

Room 30, *The Sainsbury Exhibitions Gallery*

Room 35, *The Joseph Hotung Great Court Gallery*

Changing collection displays

These are free and in Rooms 3, 69a, 90 and 91. See the screens in the Great Court for the latest information.

Please check with the Information Desk in the Great Court for opening times of Rooms 16, 20a, 33a, 77 and 78.

Gallery talks

Free 45-minute talks by a guest speaker or curator. Tue–Sat at 13.15. See the digital screens for more details.

Highlight tours (£)

Available every Fri, Sat and Sun at 11.30 and 14.00 (90 minutes). Book at the Ticket Desk in the Great Court.

Eye-opener tours

Free daily tours (30–40 minutes) introducing areas of the collection:

11.00	Japan, Room 92
11.15	Gods and goddesses of Roman Britain, Room 49
11.30	Ancient Greece, Room 17
11.45	Ancient Iraq, Room 56
12.00	Africa, Room 24
12.15	China, Room 33
12.30	The Enlightenment Gallery, Room 1
12.45	South Asia, Room 33
13.00	Mexico, Room 24
14.00	Art of the Middle East, Room 34
14.15	The world of money, Room 68
14.30	Ancient Egypt, Room 64
14.45	Medieval Europe, Room 41
15.15	Ancient Rome, Room 70
15.45	Assyrian reliefs, Room 6

Spotlight tours

Free tours (20 minutes) on Friday evenings. Ask at the Information Desk for times, topics and locations.

Hands on desks

Handle objects daily at 11.00–16.00 in Rooms 1, 2, 24, 33, 49 and 68. During exhibition runs in Room 30, there will be a handling desk outside the exhibition space.

Audio and family guide (£)

The Museum's audio guide helps you make the most of your visit. Find out more about the Museum's most popular objects or take a themed tour – it's up to you.

Available in 10 languages: English, Korean, French, German, Italian, Spanish, Arabic, Russian, Japanese and Mandarin, as well as British Sign Language and audio description.

Visiting as a family?

Explore the collection through a series of special adventures with our digital family guide. *Sponsored by Korean Air.*

Families

Free family resources
Start your adventure at the Families Desk. On weekends and school holidays pick up a Museum explorer trail to discover the collection together, or borrow a backpack full of activities to use in the galleries.

Family events
Enjoy free family activities all year round. Drop in to a weekend digital workshop or get creative with hands-on holiday activities when school's out.

Pushchairs
All our galleries are accessible and you can leave a fold-up buggy free of charge in the cloakroom during your visit.

Family eating
If you have a packed lunch, you can eat it in the Ford Centre for Young Visitors on weekends and school holidays.

Eating and shopping

Court Café
Enjoy a range of freshly made baguettes, toasted sandwiches, salads, soup and cakes in the Great Court.

Gallery Café
A relaxed family café serving sandwiches, soups, salads and pizzas.

Great Court Restaurant
Casual contemporary dining. Open daily for light morning snacks, lunch and afternoon tea. Enjoy dinner and live music on Fridays from 17.30.

Shopping
Maps, books, gifts, jewellery, replicas and children's items are sold at shops throughout the Museum. Shop online at britishmuseum.org/shop

Membership

Loved your visit today?
Become a Member and enjoy great benefits all year:

- unlimited free entry to all exhibitions
- extensive range of Members-only events
- access to the Members' Room
- regular mailings including *British Museum Magazine* three times a year
- 10% discount in British Museum shops and cafés
- free cloakroom for Members

Three ways to join:
britishmuseum.org/membership
+44 (0)20 7323 8195
Visit the Membership Desk in the Great Court

Africa

The diverse cultural life of Africa has been expressed through everyday objects and unique works of art since the beginning of human time. The African continent has provided archaeologists with the earliest examples of human activity. The Museum's collection of over 200,000 African items encompasses archaeological and contemporary material from across the continent.

Over the centuries, the close proximities and complex histories of different communities has resulted in a wide variety of regional and local styles. Differing techniques and styles emphasise the cultural, ethnic, geographical, artistic and historical diversity of Africa. The work of many contemporary artists, created both within and outside the continent, echoes the continuing significance of ancient African traditions.

Africa

The Sainsbury African Galleries
Room 25
Lower floor, Level -2

This room provides an insight into aspects of the cultural life of Africa, past and present and includes artefacts drawn from the entire continent and from many historical periods. It also features important works by some of Africa's foremost contemporary artists, as well as films demonstrating the dynamism and continuity of cultural traditions as they are enacted in Africa today.

The galleries are arranged thematically, starting with a changing display of contemporary African art and including sections on smithing and pottery, forged metal, woodcarving, masquerade, textiles and brass casting.

Figure (*nkisi*) of a dog
The wooden carving of the double-headed dog Kozo was used in rituals to solve problems or gain wealth. Packs of medicinal materials are attached to the animal's back, and nails have been driven into the figure to seek help in pursuing wrongdoers.
From Democratic Republic of Congo (formerly Zaire), about AD 1900. L 64 cm

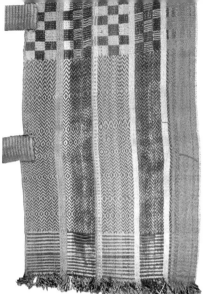

Silk hanging
Christianity has been the main religion of Ethiopia since the AD 300s. During this time the Ethiopian church has woven silk to make many beautiful objects – most impressive of all are the wall hangings.
From Magdala, Ethiopia, late AD 1700

Throne of Weapons (2001)
This was made by the Mozambican artist Cristovao (Kester) Canhavato (b. 1966) from decommissioned foreign weapons collected since the end of Mozambique's civil war in 1992. It is a vivid reminder of the damage caused in Africa by the global arms trade as well as a symbol of hope for the future as the objects of war are recycled.
From Maputo, Mozambique. H 1.01 m

Man's Cloth (2001)
This piece by the artist El Anatsui (b. 1944), is made from strips of recycled tin foil liquor bottle-top wrappers. The artist draws inspiration from the famous narrow-strip woven textiles of the Ewe and Asante people of Ghana, but also from the wider tradition of narrow-strip weaving throughout West Africa.
From Nsukka, Nigeria. H 2.97 m

Sudanese slit drum

This buffalo-shaped wooden drum was probably originally made in what is today Uganda. It is of a type used by Central-African peoples to signify the authority of local chiefs. It was probably taken north during the slave-raiding expeditions, operating out of Khartoum, which had preyed upon this part of Africa since the 1820s.

From Khartoum, Sudan, late AD 1800s. W 2.71 m

The Luzira Head

This hollow terracotta head, probably of a woman, is from the Luzira collection which consists of over 100 pieces excavated from a Baganda shrine site around 1930. The head is formed from a pot constructed using the coiling technique, a popular means of making domestic pottery.

From Luzira, Uganda, probably AD 900–1100. H 17 cm

Benin ivory mask

This mask made by Edo peoples was worn by the *Oba* (king) of Benin, probably around his neck, during a ceremony to drive away evil forces. It is said to represent Queen Mother Idia, mother of Oba Esigie, who ruled in the 16th century and established the special place of the Queen Mother in Benin society.

From Benin, Nigeria, probably AD 1500s. L 24 cm

The Ife Head
This striking brass sculpture represents an *oni* (ruler) from Ife, capital state of the Yoruba peoples, on the River Niger in south-western Nigeria. The head was probably used in funerary ceremonies and may have been attached to a wooden figure.
From Ife, Nigeria, probably AD 1300–1400s. H 35 cm

Asante state sword
It is not known when swords were introduced into the area now known as Ghana, but early examples probably derive from Islamic weapons that were passed down the trans-Saharan trade routes.
From Ghana, AD 1800s. L 70 cm

Americas

The indigenous peoples of the Americas have thrived for more than 15,000 years. At the time of European contact in AD 1492 there were more than 50 million people living from the Arctic Circle in the North to Patagonia in the South. Disease and cultural oppression have since decimated populations and threatened their cultural survival.

However, today thousands of indigenous societies have endured these challenges maintaining their vibrant traditions and diverse cultures. The comprehensive Americas collections here at the British Museum capture and express the narratives of humanity from North, Central and South America.

Americas
North America

Room 26
Ground floor, Level 0
11,000 BC–present

This room explores both historic objects and the contemporary art of the native inhabitants of Canada and the United States, while illustrating the effect of European contact and colonisation on their communities.

Objects on display range from pipes in the form of animals made by the Hopewell people in 200 BC, to warrior shirts from the AD 1800s. Textiles, clothing, carved posts and pottery are also on display. The breadth of material exhibited emphasises the vibrancy of ancient traditions, as well as the vitality of artists working today.

Zoomorphic stone pipe
Excavations in Ohio have uncovered superbly carved pipes and other exotic trade goods and fine artworks. This pipe is in the shape of an otter and may have been smoked for purification during rituals.
From Mound City, Ohio, North America, 200 BC–AD 100. H 5 cm

Warrior shirt

This shirt belonged to the Kainai chief, Red Crow, a successful warrior who won several battles. The shirt shows evidence of trade between Native Americans and Europeans; the glass beads originate from Venice, Italy or Bohemia, Czech Republic and the red collar is made from wool that probably came from Gloucestershire, England.
From Alberta, Canada, probably mid AD 1800s. L 1 m

Mask of the *Nulthamalth*

The right to wear certain masks is a proud inheritance of Kwakwaka'wakw chiefs. Masks can represent powerful beings and are worn and danced at ceremonies known as potlatches. This is the mask of the *Nulthamalth*, or fool dancer.
From British Columbia, Canada, AD 1800s. H 33 cm

Clovis point

Clovis spear points are the best archaeological evidence for the earliest settlement of North America so far discovered. The people who made Clovis points possibly migrated across Beringia, the land bridge that once connected Siberia to Alaska.
From Arizona, North America, about 11,000 BC. H 3 cm

Americas
Mexico

Room 27
Ground floor, Level 0
About 2000 BC–AD 1500s

This room is organised geographically to reflect the distinctive regional cultures that flourished in Mexico from about 2000 BC up to the time of European contact in the AD 1500s. Mexica (Aztec) civilisation is explored, along with the Classic Veracruz and Huaxtec cultures and the Maya city states of AD 1–1000. The display includes highly-prized turquoise mosaics, dating from the Mixtec culture of AD 1400–1521, and stone sculptures of Huaxtec female deities from AD 900–1450.

Huaxtec goddess sculpture
When the Aztecs conquered the Huaxtec in around AD 1450, they identified the Huaxtec mother-goddess with their earth goddess Tlazolteotl. Fertility is a recurring theme in Huaxtec art, represented by stone sculptures of female goddesses, elderly men and phalluses.
From the Pánuco River region, Mexico, AD 900–1521. H 1.5 m

Double-headed serpent mosaic
An icon of Mexica art, this turquoise mosaic was probably worn on ceremonial occasions as a pectoral (an ornament worn on the chest). Serpent imagery occurs throughout the religious iconography of Mexico and Central America, and is associated with several Mexica deities.
From Mexico, AD 1400s–1500s.
H 20 cm

Gold pendant figurine
This pendant represents a Mixtec nobleman wearing a necklace, earrings and a lip plug from which hangs a mask with three suspended bells. He carries a staff in his right hand and a shield in the left. Pendants similar to this one were used as burial offerings.
From Tehuantepec, Oaxaca, Mexico, AD 900–1521.
H 8 cm

Yaxchilán lintel
This limestone relief is considered one of the masterpieces of Mayan art. It shows the king of Yaxchilán, Shield Jaguar the Great (r. AD 681–742) holding a flaming torch over his wife, who is pulling a thorny rope through her tongue during a bloodletting ritual.
From Yaxchilán, Mexico, about AD 723–726. H 1.09 m

Ancient Egypt

The collection from ancient Egypt and Sudan illustrates every aspect of the ancient Nile Valley culture from Neolithic times (about 10,000 BC), down to Late Antiquity when Christianity became the main religion in Egypt (around AD 400–800).

Egypt became the greatest and most enduring of African kingdoms, despite periods of internal breakdown and foreign invasion. Agricultural prosperity, dependent on the annual inundation of the Nile, provided Egypt with a stable foundation, and under the rule of the pharaohs, a strong centralised state developed. The early introduction of writing, the mastery of building and carving in stone, and a sophisticated religion with elaborate treatment of the dead all became defining features of this highly organised society.

Ancient Egypt
Egyptian sculpture

Room 4
Ground floor, Level 0
2570 BC–AD 100

Ancient Egyptian civilisation lasted for over 3000 years. The sculpture in this gallery is laid out broadly chronologically, from the Old Kingdom up to Roman rule. The displays are presented in their social, religious and historical contexts.

Monumental sculpture was a key element of Egyptian temples and tombs. The statues and reliefs are idealised images that served as vehicles for the spirits of deities, kings and privileged officials. The room also features architectural pieces and large sarcophagi, including one made for Egypt's last pharaoh.

The Rosetta Stone
The Rosetta Stone bears a text in Egyptian hieroglyphs, demotic and Greek and its discovery enabled the modern decipherment of Egypt's ancient pictographic script. The text is a decree from a council of priests affirming the royal cult of King Ptolemy V.
From Egypt, 196 BC.
H 1.12 m

Statue of Ramesses II
The largest Egyptian statue
in the British Museum
represents Ramesses II,
whose prosperous reign
lasted almost 67 years.
*From Thebes, Egypt,
about 1250 BC. H 2.67 m*

Head of Amenhotep III
King Amenhotep III
commissioned numerous
statues of himself, especially
for his temples in Thebes, then
Egypt's capital. In this granite
statue he wears the double
crown of Upper and Lower
Egypt. An arm of the same
statue is also on display.
*From Thebes, Egypt, about
1370 BC. H 2.87 m*

List of kings (detail)
This limestone list of Egyptian rulers comes from a
temple of Ramesses II. Lists of this kind are important
for chronology, but also inform us about Egyptian
ideas of history.
From Abydos, Egypt, about 1250 BC. H 1.35 m

Ancient Egypt
Egyptian life and death

The Michael Cohen Gallery
Room 61
Upper floors, Level 3
1400–1300 BC

This room includes remarkable wall-paintings from the tomb of a rich accountant named Nebamun in the Temple of Amun at Thebes (modern Karnak). His tomb was constructed around 1350 BC and the chapel was decorated with extraordinarily beautiful paintings showing an idealised vision of life for eternity. Other objects in the gallery hint at the actual experience of living in Egypt for both rich and poor.

Tomb-painting of a hunt in the marshes
Here Nebamun is shown hunting birds, in a small boat with his wife Hatshepsut and their young daughter. Following Egyptian stylistic traditions, as the most important person in the image, Nebamun is shown as the largest figure and occupies the centre of the scene. The hieroglyphs say that the dead tomb-owner is 'enjoying himself and seeing beauty'.
From Thebes, Egypt, about 1350 BC. H 83 cm

Ancient Egypt
Egyptian death and afterlife: mummies

The Roxie Walker Galleries
Rooms 62–63
Upper floors, Level 3
About 2686 BC–AD 395

Death and the afterlife held particular significance and meaning for the ancient Egyptians. Complex funeral preparations and rites were thought to be needed to ensure the transition of the individual from earthly existence to immortality.

Objects on display include coffins, mummies, funerary masks, portraits and other items designed to be buried with the deceased. To ensure a successful afterlife for the dead through mummification, most of their internal organs were removed and preserved in distinctive jars. The brain was also removed, but not preserved, and the rest of the body was packed with natural salt and tightly wrapped in bandages. Small figures called *shabtis* were also buried to magically provide for the deceased. A range of animals sacred to the gods – such as bulls, crocodiles, cats and falcons – were also mummified.

Book of the Dead of Hunefer
The *Book of the Dead* is a collection of spells to guide the dead through the netherworld. This papyrus sheet shows the judgement of the dead in the presence of Osiris and the weighing of the heart.
From Thebes, Egypt, about 1290 BC. H 39 cm

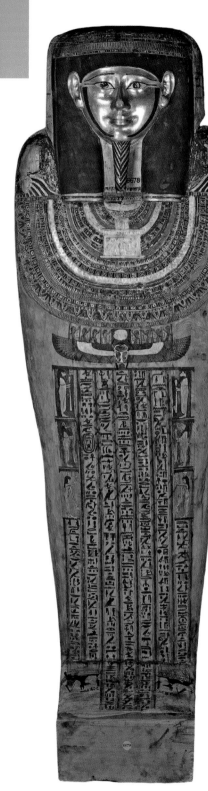

Blue-glazed *shabti* of Sety I
Shabti figures were part of
ancient Egyptian funerary
traditions. The *shabti* spell
from the *Book of the Dead*
indicated that the *shabtis*
must do the work of its
owner in the afterlife. This
is one of the finest of the
many faience *shabtis* found
in the tomb of Sety I.
*From the Valley of the Kings,
Egypt, about 1290 BC.
H 23 cm*

Inner coffin of Hornedjitef
The mummy of the priest
Hornedjitef was encased in a
gilded mask and cover, and two
human-shaped wooden coffins.
This is the delicately decorated
inner-coffin.
*From Thebes, Egypt,
300–200 BC. L 1.94 m*

Mummy of a cat

Animals associated with deities were regularly mummified in the later periods of Egyptian history. The cat is associated with the goddess Bastet, whose cult centre was at Bubastis in the Delta, but there were other feline deities elsewhere in Egypt.

From Abydos, Egypt,
perhaps AD 1–100. L 46 cm

Wooden stela of Nakhtefmut

During the Third Intermediate Period (about 1070–664 BC) wooden stelae were placed in tombs with the deceased. These stelae are usually brightly coloured and most are quite small. This example shows the owner Nakhtefmut – accompanied by his daughter Shepeniset – adoring Re-Horakhty, the falcon-headed sun-god.

Perhaps from Thebes, Egypt, about 900 BC. H 27 cm

Ancient Egypt
Early Egypt

The Raymond and Beverly Sackler Gallery
Room 64
Upper floors, Level 3
5000–2600 BC

This gallery explores the beginnings of ancient Egyptian civilisation, which developed along the Nile around 5000 BC. Rapid advances in technology and social organisation during this period produced a material culture of increasing sophistication.

Further innovations followed in about 3100 BC when the separate Predynastic peoples of Upper (southern) and Lower (northern) Egypt were united under a single ruler. The resulting increase in wealth and strong central control led to dramatic achievements in architecture, writing and fine goods, culminating in the building of the Great Pyramid of Giza in around 2600 BC. Objects on display illustrate the cultural, technological and political development of early civilisation in Egypt throughout this period.

Ivory label for King Den's sandals
One of the king's main duties was to defend and expand Egypt's frontiers. King Den is shown here about to strike a Bedouin representative with a mace. Most ivory plaques dating to the First Dynasty were made as labels. The pair of sandals incised on the back of this one indicates that it was a label for sandals, which were extremely prestigious items.
From Abydos, Egypt, about 2985 BC. H 5 cm

Mudstone palette

Palettes were used for grinding cosmetics and were often decorated. They were also used to commemorate events, or to display the power of leading figures. It is assumed that this palette represents a battlefield, with enemies fallen in battle. It is possible that the lion signifies a ruler or king, and that the palette records a royal victory.

From Abydos, Egypt, about 3150 BC. L 28 cm

Pottery group of cattle

Cattle were revered in Egypt and were worshipped as the cow goddess Bat – the protector and mother of the pharaoh. This model of four cows shows the earliest domestic cattle in Africa. They are from over 5000 years ago, from a time when Egypt was populated by small farming communities along the Nile Valley.

From el-Amra, Egypt, about 3500 BC. H 10 cm

Bone figure of a woman

Figures such as this were found in graves and are thought to have provided magical support for the owner's rebirth and regeneration. The large and striking eyes are inlaid with lapis lazuli, witness to the extensive trade network that must have existed at this date, for the nearest lapis lazuli quarries are found in modern-day Afghanistan.

From Upper Egypt, 4000–3600 BC. H 11 cm

Ancient Egypt
Sudan, Egypt and Nubia

The Raymond and Beverly Sackler Gallery
Room 65
Upper floors, Level 3
Palaeolithic–AD 1000s

Ancient Nubia – the Nile Valley upstream of the First Cataract – now straddles the border between Egypt and Sudan. Rich and vibrant cultures developed in this region at the same time as Pharaonic Egypt. Among them was the earliest sub-Saharan urban culture in Africa, which was based at Kerma (modern Sudan). These cultures traded extensively with Egypt and for two brief periods, Nubian kingdoms dominated their northern neighbour.

Pottery beaker
The cultures of Kerma flourished between about 2500 and 1500 BC. Their potters were able to produce incredibly fine vessels by hand, without using a wheel. The pot shown here, belonging to the so-called 'Classic Kerma' phase, is characterised by a black top and a rich red-brown body, separated by an irregular purple-grey band.
From Kerma, Sudan,
about 1750–1450 BC. H 11 cm

Sphinx of King Taharqo
This sphinx represents Taharqo, the fourth Kushite pharaoh from Sudan to rule Egypt. The Kushites conquered Egypt in around 720 BC and adopted Egyptian iconography to govern their new empire. Although the general form of the sphinx is typical of Egyptian sculpture, it is adorned with a Kushite headdress and the face is carved in a Kushite style.
From Kawa, Sudan,
about 680 BC. L 73 cm

Egypt was one of the first countries in which Christianity flourished – later spreading to Nubia (modern Sudan) and Ethiopia – and was the birthplace of monasticism. The word 'Copt', derived from the Greek name for Egyptians (*Aigyptioi*), is now used to describe the country's Christian population, but originally referred to all Egyptians. Objects produced during this period in Egypt and Nubia may have featured distinctive Christian images, but also motifs from earlier Pharaonic Egypt, and from the art, architecture and mythology of Greece and Rome.

Ethiopia, said by outsiders to be a fabled land controlling the flow of the Nile, was also on a major trade route, linking Egypt and the Mediterranean with India and the Far East. The resulting history of cultural exchange and religious diversity is illustrated through objects in this room that reflect the faiths and identities that coexisted in Egypt, Nubia and Ethiopia.

Wall-painting of the martyrdom of saints
This wall-painting is composed of two distinct scenes. The central panel shows three Hebrew saints in the furnace. This scene was later framed by five Christian saints, martyred during the persecution of the Roman emperor Diocletian in the late AD 200s.
From Wadi Sarga, Egypt, AD 500–699. L 1.44 m

Ancient Greece and Rome

The Greek and Roman galleries display objects from the Bronze Age until the fall of Rome (about 3200 BC to AD 476). They show the expansion of the Greek world across the Mediterranean and beyond, the growth of increasingly powerful Italian cultures, and their coming together in the Roman Empire (for Roman Britain, see pp. 88–89 in the Europe section).

The displays of Greek art span over 1500 years. They illustrate the development of sophisticated ceramics, showing scenes from myth and daily life, and the emergence of realism in sculpting the human form.

Ancient Greece and Rome
Greece: Cycladic Islands

Room 11
Ground floor, Level 0
3200–1250 BC

During the early part of the Greek Bronze Age (3200–1500 BC), the people of the Aegean islands – known as the Cyclades – began to produce metal goods from copper, silver and lead, and other objects from the fine white marble of the area. Objects on display include marble vessels and the Cycladic figurines. Trade and outside influences increased during the Bronze Age, but pottery continued to be produced in a distinctive Cycladic style.

Marble figurine of a woman
This unusually large Cycladic 'folded-arm' figurine is very well-preserved, with traces of painted eyes and jewellery. The function and meaning of these figurines is not known but they were often found in graves.
From the Cyclades, Aegean Sea, about 2600–2400 BC. H 77 cm

Ancient Greece and Rome
Greece: Minoan Crete and Mycenaeans

The Arthur I Fleischman Gallery
Room 12
Ground floor, Level 0
3200–1100 BC

Minoan and Mycenaean are the terms used to describe the Bronze Age societies of Crete and mainland Greece. Minoan Crete was dominated by large, complex buildings called 'palaces' which acted as administrative, agricultural and religious centres.

The Mycenaean period of the Late Bronze Age (1600–1100 BC) was viewed by the Greeks as the 'Age of Heroes' and perhaps provides the historical background to many of the stories told in later Greek mythology, including Homer's epics.

Gold pendant from the Aigina treasure
This Minoan figure holds a waterfowl in each hand, with stylised plants behind. The pose is known as the 'Master of the Animals' and is found in other Mediterranean cultures.
Found on Aigina, Greece, made about 1850–1550 BC. H 6 cm

Minoan bull and acrobat
This bronze figurine depicts a man somersaulting over a bull. Bulls were the largest animals on Crete and were of great significance in Minoan society. Bull-leaping was part of an organised performance, although the style of leap depicted here is almost impossible.
From Crete, about 1700–1450 BC. H 11 cm

Ancient Greece and Rome
Greece 1050–520 BC

Room 13
Ground floor, Level 0

The period following the collapse of the Mycenaean kingdoms saw profound changes in Greek society and culture. After an initial decline in living standards, powerful independent city-states emerged. From the 8th century BC onwards, renewed contact with other peoples around the Mediterranean, in the Near East, Anatolia, Phoenicia and Egypt brought new wealth and cultural influences.

On display here you'll see sculpture, painted pottery, jewellery, coins and other objects from Greek cities and regions such as Athens, Sparta, Corinth and Boeotia, and Greek trading posts such as Naukratis in Egypt.

Amphora depicting Achilles
This exquisitely painted amphora (wine-jar) is signed by Exekias, one of the most skilful of Athenian potters and painters. It shows Achilles looming above the Amazon Queen Penthesilea: their eyes meet and they fall in love just as he delivers the blow that kills her. Penthesilea had brought her female warriors to help the Trojans defend their city, but was defeated by Achilles, the greatest of the Greek warriors.
Made in Athens, Greece, about 540–530 BC, found at Vulci, Italy. H 41 cm

The Sophilos Dinos

This is the earliest Greek vessel with a painter's signature, in this case Sophilos. Bowls for mixing wine and water were used in the Greek *symposion* (communal drinking party). The elaborate mythical wedding procession (of Peleus and Thetis, the starting point of the story of the Trojan War) on this bowl shows the new direction in which Athenian vase painting was moving, away from the animal friezes of earlier Corinthian and East Greek vase paintings.
From Athens, Greece, about 580 BC. H 71 cm

Gold coin of Croesus

King of the Lydian people (r. about 560–547 BC), Croesus was renowned for his great wealth. The earliest coins issued in gold have often been attributed to Croesus. His royal capital was at the city of Sardis, in what is now central Turkey. It stood on the River Pactolus where electrum, an alloy of gold and silver, occurs naturally in the sands of the river bed. Gold and silver were also found nearby and were used widely in coinage.
From Lydia, now Turkey, about 550 BC. H 10 mm

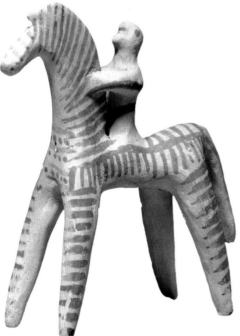

Terracotta horse and horseman

Horse and rider figures were popular grave offerings in 6th-century Boeotia. It is likely that the possession of a real horse was a mark of social and even political status.
From Tanagra, Boeotia, Greece, about 550 BC. H 13 cm

Ancient Greece and Rome
Greek vases

Rooms 14 and 20a
Ground floor, Level 0
550–300 BC

The British Museum's collection of ancient Greek painted pottery is one of the largest and finest in the world. Examples can be found throughout the ancient Greek galleries of the Museum.

Fine pottery was produced across the Greek world, including in the Greek settlements in Italy. It had many different functions, practical and ritual, at home, in sanctuaries and in cemeteries. Athens was the leading producer of painted pottery from around 580 until 300 BC, and its products were popular all over the Mediterranean region.

Though not considered 'artists' in ancient times, many potters and painters were highly gifted and innovative, and some gained a certain status and wealth. Their experiments led to a new style of decoration, the red-figure technique (red figures against a black background) replacing the earlier black-figure style and becoming common across the Greek world from around 500 BC.

Amphora depicting Herakles
This elegant two-handled amphora (wine jar) is exceptional because it combines the traditional black-figure with the new red-figure style of painting. On one side the heroes Ajax and Achilles appear in black on an orange-red background, on the other side the hero Herakles is throwing a lion over his shoulder, and the colour scheme is reversed.
Made in Attica, Greece, 520–500 BC.
H 55 cm

Amphora depicting Dionysos and two satyrs

This black-figured neck-amphora shows Dionysos, the god of wine, holding a drinking-horn in one hand and a vine branch in the other. The other side depicts a four-horse chariot.

Made in Athens, Greece, about 530–520 BC, found at Vulci, Italy. H 40 cm

Lekythos depicting Odysseus

This lekythos (oil or perfume jar) shows Odysseus escaping from the cave of the Cyclops Polyphemos, the terrible, one-eyed, man-eating giant.

Made in Athens, Greece, about 480 BC, found at Vulci, Italy. H 15 cm

Ancient Greece and Rome
Athens and Lycia

Room 15
Ground floor, Level 0
520–430 BC

Following the defeat of the Persian invasion of Greece in 480–479 BC, Athens took the lead in a defence league of Greek states, which soon turned into a powerful (and increasingly oppressive) maritime empire. In an age of prosperity, Athenian arts and craft flourished and a democratic system was developed in which all male citizens, rich or poor, shared political power, but which excluded women, foreigners and slaves.

Among those pressed into joining Athens as allies and paying tribute were the Lycians, living in what is now south-west Turkey.

Tomb of King Kybernis
This is the tomb of the warrior-king Kybernis of Xanthos in Lycia. It was carved in the shape of a house on a pillar and richly decorated with reliefs. Kybernis led the Lycian ships in the Persian invasion of Greece in 480 BC but the style of the sculpture shows strong Greek influence.
From Xanthos, Turkey, about 470–460 BC. H 8.84 m

Ancient Greece and Rome
Greece: Bassai sculptures

This room displays a rare example of an almost-complete architectural frieze from the ancient Greek world. Made between 429 and 400 BC, the frieze ran around the interior of the Temple of Apollo at Bassai in Greece. The frieze shows scenes of two battles, between the Greeks and the Amazons, and a tribe of northern Greek Lapiths fighting centaurs.

The Bassai Frieze
This section of the marble frieze shows Herakles and other Greeks fighting the Amazons.
From Bassai, Arcadia, Greece, about 420–400 BC. L 1.78 m

Ancient Greece and Rome
Nereid Monument

Room 17
Ground floor, Level 0
390–380 BC

The Nereid Monument is the largest and finest of the Lycian tombs found at Xanthos (modern Turkey). It was built for Erbinna, ruler of Xanthos. Although he was not Greek, Erbinna chose to be buried in a tomb that resembles a Greek temple.

Its lavish decorative sculpture, which can be seen reconstructed and displayed around the walls of the gallery, is a mixture of Greek and Lycian style and iconography. Persian influences are also apparent in the dress of some of the figures, notably Erbinna himself.

The original position of many of the sculptures is open to question and the reconstruction shown here is disputed.

The Nereid Monument
The monument takes its name from the Nereids, mythical sea-nymphs and daughters of the sea-god Nereus, whose statues were placed between the columns of this monumental tomb.
From Xanthos, Turkey, 390–380 BC.

Frieze from the Nereid Monument
Both Greek and Middle Eastern ideas are combined in this marble frieze from the base of the monument. It shows the enthroned Lycian ruler dressed like a Persian king, shaded by a parasol, while his army and the audience he receives are dressed in Greek style.
From Xanthos, Turkey, 390–380 BC.
L 1.2 m

Ancient Greece and Rome
Greece: Parthenon

Room 18
Ground floor, Level 0
447–432 BC

The Parthenon on the Acropolis at Athens was built between 447 and 438 BC as a temple dedicated to Athena, patron goddess of the city. The temple's great size and lavish use of white marble was intended to show off the city's power and wealth at the height of its empire. The temple was richly decorated with sculptures representing scenes from mythology and cult: the frieze (carved in low relief) ran around all four sides of the building inside the colonnade. Metopes (rectangular slabs carved in high relief) were placed above the architrave on the outside of the temple and sculptures, carved in the round, filled the gables at either end. The pediments and metopes illustrate episodes from Greek mythology, while the frieze represents the people of contemporary Athens in religious procession.

Sculpture of Ilissos
This reclining figure from the west pediment of the Parthenon represents one of the rivers of Attica, possibly the river Ilissos.
From the Acropolis, Athens, Greece, about 438–432 BC.
L 1.56 m

Metope of a centaur and Lapith

This is one of 92 metopes from the Parthenon. It shows a centaur (part man, part horse), battling with a human Lapith (member of a mythical tribe from northern Greece). The carving captures fine details of the fight and the combatants: the centaur's wrinkled nose and bared teeth add to his expression of pain and violent rage.
From the Acropolis, Athens, Greece, about 447–438 BC. L 1.32 m

Sculpture of Iris

Iris, goddess of the rainbow and divine messenger, is shown in flight. Her bronze wings, now missing, soared above her. The figure with its finely carved tunic shows the power of the great stone-workers of the Parthenon to make marble come alive.
From the Acropolis, Athens, Greece, about 438–432 BC. H 1.35 m

Sculpture of a horse's head

The chariot of the moon-goddess Selene on the east pediment of the Parthenon balanced the group of the sun-god Helios in the other corner. With its bulging eyes and stretched skin, this sculpture captures the essence of the stress felt by an animal that has spent the night drawing the chariot of the moon across the sky.
From the Acropolis, Athens, Greece, about 438–432 BC. L 83 cm

Ancient Greece and Rome
Greece: Athens

Room 19
Ground floor, Level 0
430–400 BC

For much of the 5th century BC, Athens was the premier city state in mainland Greece. The Acropolis, the sacred heart of the city, was built as a great showpiece of Athenian power, wealth and art. When the Parthenon was completed in 432 BC, Athens had already embarked on the disastrous Peloponnesian War against Sparta. Final defeat in 404 BC brought about the end of Athens' golden age and stripped the city of its empire, defences and – for a time at least – its democratic government.

The temple of Athena Nike (Victory) and the Erechtheum on the Acropolis are two buildings represented by sculpture and architecture on display. Marble grave-markers and smaller objects explore the themes of war and death.

Marble block from the Temple of Athena Nike
The temple was completed in the late 420s BC. This section from the west frieze features a battle scene between Greeks, alluding to contemporary wars.
From the Acropolis, Athens, Greece, about 425 BC.
H 44 cm

Ancient Greece and Rome
Greeks and Lycians 400–325 BC

Room 20
Ground floor, Level 0

After the defeat of Athens and the collapse of its empire in 404 BC, a power struggle on both sides of the Aegean Sea followed. In the Greek mainland the once independent city states eventually fell under the rising power of Macedon. On the other side of the Aegean, Persia reasserted its imperial power over the east-Greek cities.

Objects on display illustrate the rise in private luxury that accompanied political and social change in the 4th century BC. They include gold jewellery, exquisite metalwork showing the influence of Persian art, and a focus on novel representation of the human body.

Decorative relief
This decorative relief from a mirror cover shows Aphrodite, the goddess of love, and the Trojan Anchises reclining on Mount Ida.
From Greece, about 320 BC.
H 15 cm

Ancient Greece and Rome
Mausoleum of Halikarnassos

Room 21
Ground floor, Level 0
About 350 BC

The Mausoleum at Halikarnassos was a large and elaborate tomb built for King Maussollos and his wife Artemisia. It was worked on by several of the most distinguished Greek sculptors of the period and was considered one of the Seven Wonders of the Ancient World. The word mausoleum, now used to mean a tomb in general, was derived from this monument. Colossal free-standing statues and marble relief slabs from the Mausoleum can be seen in this room, as well as fragments of the huge marble, four-horse chariot that crowned the pyramid roof.

Marble head of Apollo
The god Apollo is shown here in a dynamic pose, with his head turned sharply, his hair windswept, his mouth slightly open and his expression exhilarated.
From Bodrum, Turkey, about 350 BC.
H 42 cm

Horse from a chariot-group
A four-horse chariot-group was positioned on the top of the stepped pyramid that crowned the Mausoleum at Halikarnassos. The chariot was perhaps driven by Maussollos himself, or a god.
From Bodrum, Turkey, about 350 BC. H 2.33 m

Ancient Greece and Rome
The world of Alexander

This room shows the Greek world when it was at its height – the age of Alexander the Great. His conquest of old empires to the east and south opened up vast new areas to the influence of Greek culture, which by the end of the period extended to southern France, north-west India and Pakistan, Egypt and southern Russia.

The Hellenistic period dates from the death of Alexander the Great in 323 BC and ends with the defeat of Cleopatra VII and Mark Antony at Actium in 31 BC. After his death, Alexander's empire was divided up into kingdoms, ruled by his generals. The major dynasties supported major architectural programmes and were great patrons of the arts and culture.

Marble column drum
This is a fragment from one of the Seven Wonders of the Ancient World, the Temple of Artemis at Ephesos. The temple was built on a massive scale after the earlier temple on the same site was destroyed by fire. It has the remains of seven figures, showing a scene presided over by the messenger god Hermes.
From Ephesos, Turkey, about 340–320 BC. H 1.84 m

Ancient Greece and Rome
Greek and Roman sculpture

Room 23
Ground floor, Level 0
100 BC–AD 200

The Roman conquest of the Greek world in the 3rd century BC brought many Greek masterpieces to Rome and subjected Roman artistic taste to the influence of Greek style. Patrons employed copyists to make replicas of their favourite works and many of the sculptures on display here are Roman versions of Greek originals made hundreds of years earlier. Many Romans believed that Greek art was superior to that of Rome, and public figures promoted their influence by adopting Greek style in the buildings and artworks they commissioned.

Statue of crouching Aphrodite
Statues of Aphrodite (Venus) were found widely in ancient Greece. All were inspired to some degree by a life-size marble sculpture made around 360 BC by the Athenian sculptor Praxiteles for the city of Knidos in present-day Turkey. Known only through Roman copies, it showed the goddess attempting to cover her nakedness.
AD 100s. H 1.12 m

Ancient Greece and Rome
Greek and Roman life

Room 69
Upper floors, Level 3
1450 BC–AD 500

Objects on display in this gallery take a cross-cultural look at daily life, both public and private in the ancient Greek and Roman world. The exhibits illustrate themes such as marriage, death, medicine, women, children, household furniture, religion, trade and transport, athletics, war, farming and many more. Around the walls supplementary displays illustrate individual crafts, on one side of the room, and Greek mythology, on the opposite side.

White-ground jug
Working wool was seen as appropriate for respectable women in ancient Greece. It was done at home and contributed to the household's wealth. This jug shows a remarkably beautiful image of a domestic chore.
Made in Athens, Greece, 490–470 BC, found at Locri, Italy. H 21 cm

Helmet of a Murmillo
Although gladiators were sometimes slaves or criminals, many were professionals who trained to be a specific type of gladiator. This bronze helmet of a Murmillo was heavy (3.5 kg); when new it had a golden sheen and was decorated with plumes.
Said to be from Pompeii, Italy, AD 1–100. H 46 cm

Ancient Greece and Rome
Roman Empire

The Wolfson Gallery
Room 70
Upper floors, Level 3
753 BC–AD 476

This gallery tells the story of Rome, which grew from a small town into the capital of an empire that ruled the Mediterranean, the Middle East and much of Europe. The gallery covers a period of approximately 1000 years from Rome's legendary foundation in 753 BC to AD 476 when Rome was conquered. By then the capital of the Roman Empire had moved to Constantinople, present-day Istanbul.

Objects on display come from all over the empire. They range from stone and metal sculptures of emperors and gods to jewellery, silverware, pottery and glass.

The Portland Vase
This is the most famous cameo-glass vessel from antiquity. The making of these vessels requires great skill and technical ability. The subject depicted here is one of love and marriage with a mythological theme and it may have been made as a wedding gift.
From Rome, Italy, about AD 5–25. H 24 cm

Marble statue of the emperor Septimius Severus
Septimius Severus (r. AD 193–211) was the first Roman emperor born in Africa. He is shown with his characteristic forked beard and tightly curled hair and is wearing military dress. Like many emperors he was quite cosmopolitan and well-travelled: he was born in Libya, had a Syrian wife and campaigned throughout the empire before dying in York, England.
Found at Alexandria, Egypt, made about AD 193–200. H 1.98 m

Head of Augustus (The Meroë Head)

This bronze head once formed part of a statue of the emperor Augustus (r. 27 BC–AD 14). It is likely that the head was looted from southern Egypt when the neighbouring Kushites invaded. It was deliberately buried beneath the steps of a temple dedicated to the goddess Victory as a sign of triumph over the Roman Empire.

From Meroë, Sudan, about 27–25 BC. H 46 cm

The Warren Cup

This is a Roman silver cup with relief decoration featuring two scenes of men making love. Made in Hellenistic style, probably in and for a Greek part of the Empire. The Romans had no concept of, or word for, homosexuality, while in the Greek world the partnering of older men with youths was an accepted element of society within certain parameters. The cup reflects the customs and attitudes of this historical context.

Said to be from Battir, near Jerusalem, AD 5–15. H 11 cm

Ancient Greece and Rome
Etruscan world

Before the Roman Empire, Italy was home to many different cultures, including the Etruscans who inhabited part of western central Italy. The Etruscans flourished between the 8th and 1st centuries BC and grew wealthy from mining, agriculture and trading throughout the Mediterranean. They were famed in antiquity for being devoutly religious, for their metalworking, their love of music and banqueting, and the independence they allowed their women.

The Etruscans heavily influenced Roman culture, but by 200 BC, like the rest of Italy, they had fallen under Roman rule. The wide range of objects in this room illustrate life and beliefs in pre-Roman Italy.

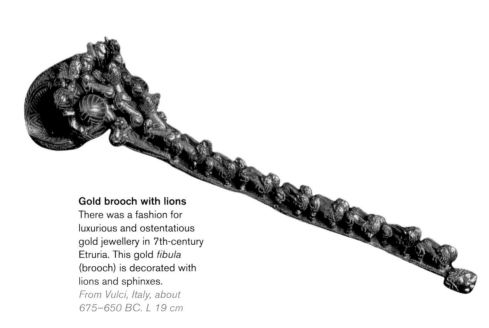

Gold brooch with lions
There was a fashion for luxurious and ostentatious gold jewellery in 7th-century Etruria. This gold *fibula* (brooch) is decorated with lions and sphinxes.
From Vulci, Italy, about 675–650 BC. L 19 cm

Ancient Greece and Rome
Ancient Cyprus

The A G Leventis Gallery
Room 72
Upper floors, Level 3
4500 BC–AD 330

The island of Cyprus, in Greek mythology the land of Aphrodite, goddess of love and sex, has been inhabited for at least 12,000 years. Settlers were attracted by its wildlife (for hunting) and fertile land, and traders by its abundant resources of timber and copper. The word copper actually comes from the name Cyprus. Over the centuries, major political powers fought for control over Cyprus, because of its strategic location in the eastern Mediterranean. This long history of contact created a material culture that was eclectic, yet still distinctively Cypriot. The objects on display were all made or found on Cyprus and illustrate Cypriot culture and civilisation from the 4th millennium BC to the end of the Roman period.

Woman with child
The human form was represented in Cypriot art from the earliest times, but the first figures were abstract, in contrast with the realism of later Greek sculpture on the island. 'Plank figurines' such as this terracotta example are usually interpreted as either a mother goddess or a mortal woman with child. They are probably connected with fertility, childbirth and sexuality.
From Cyprus, about 1975–1850 BC.
H 26 cm

Ancient Greece and Rome
Greeks in Italy

Room 73
Upper floors, Level 3
750–250 BC

Trade and the search for raw materials, especially metals, first brought the ancient Greeks to southern Italy and Sicily from around 750 BC. Sometimes this led to permanently settled outposts, populated initially by Greeks.

The wide range of objects on display in this gallery, including pottery, jewellery and coins, demonstrate the many connections across the Greek world. From around 250 BC Rome had taken firm control of the Greek south, but in so doing it also absorbed much of Greek culture and its artistic skills bringing Greek language, writing, arts, craftsmanship and religion to Italy.

Silver *decadrachm* of Syracuse
Some of the finest Sicilian coins, like this silver *decadrachm*, are from the city of Syracuse. These coins have often been interpreted as presentation pieces struck in commemoration of the Syracusan victory over the Athenians in the Peloponnesian War in 413 BC.
From Syracuse, Sicily, about 413 BC. Diam. 35 mm

**Bronze statuette of
a warrior on horseback**
This is one of the earliest pieces of
'Western Greek' (made in Italy under
Greek influence) sculpture to survive.
Although it is small, the horse and
rider have a monumental quality which
seems to give them dignity and status.
*From Armento, Italy, about 560–550
BC. H 24 cm*

Volute-krater
Large pottery vessels were popular grave
gifts in the Greek cities of southern Italy.
They often display mythological scenes
inspired by theatre or relating to death and
the afterlife, such as here, the sacrifice
of young Iphigeneia, an episode from
the Trojan War that was dramatised by
Euripides in 413 BC.
*Found in Basilicata, Italy, made 370–350
BC. H 69 cm*

Gold *phiale*
This shallow gold bowl is decorated
with six bulls in relief, and was used as a
libation bowl for making liquid offerings
to the gods. It was found in a tomb
in Sicily and although it is probably a
Greek product, its style betrays strong
Phoenician influence.
*Found in Sant'Angelo Muxaro, Sicily,
made about 600 BC. Diam. 15 cm*

Ancient Greece and Rome
Greek and Roman architecture

Room 77
Lower floor, Level -1
530 BC–AD 300

The British Museum has an especially important collection of architectural fragments and sculpture from ancient Greek and Roman buildings. These provided the template for the revival of Classical architecture in Europe from the time of the Renaissance.

Fragments of buildings on display here include the earlier and later temples of Artemis at Ephesos, the Propylaea (gateway), Erechtheum and temple of Athena Nike from the Acropolis of Athens, the temple of Apollo at Bassai, the Mausoleum at Halikarnassos and the temple of Athena Polias at Priene. Examples of Roman architecture show the development of new orders.

Lion's head spout
Artemis Ephesia, an Anatolian fertility goddess, was worshipped on the same site at Ephesos for a long period. The 6th-century version of the temple was built with funds from the Lydian king Croesus.
From Ephesos, Turkey, 400–300 BC.
L 53 cm

Ancient Greece and Rome
Classical inscriptions

Room 78
Lower floor, Level -1
600 BC–AD 300

Ancient Greek and Roman inscriptions are displayed in this room and show how script engraved in stone was used to record and commemorate events and transactions. These include examples of civic or official inscriptions such as laws, decrees, treaties and accounts of income and expenditure from public funds. In the private sphere, inscriptions on gravestones served to commemorate the dead. Many bear poignant epitaphs of remembrance.

Defaced dedicatory inscription
The inscription on this marble altar records that it was dedicated by Antonius, a *libertus* or freed slave, and commemorates the safe return of the emperor Septimius Severus (r. AD 193–211), his wife Julia Domna, their children Geta and Caracalla, and Caracalla's wife, Plautilla. Caracalla became emperor and murdered his brother, a possible rival, and executed his own wife, after reported plotting. Geta and Plautilla suffered the *damnatio memoriae*, or condemnation of their memory, hence their names were erased from any inscription.
From Rome, Italy, AD 193–211. H 81 cm

Asia

The British Museum holds one of the richest collections of Chinese antiquities in Europe, containing many examples of Chinese painting, calligraphy, jades, bronzes and ceramics. The Chinese collection ranges from 4000 BC to the present.

The Japanese collections are particularly strong in paintings, prints and decorative arts from AD 1600 to the present.

The sculpture collection from the Indian sub-continent is the most representative in the west.

Asia
China, South Asia and Southeast Asia

The Joseph E Hotung Gallery of Oriental Antiquities
Room 33
Ground floor, Level 1
Paleolithic–present

This room explores the history of the material and visual cultures of China, South and Southeast Asia, from prehistoric times to the present day through objects of daily use, works of art, religious images and finds from tombs and hoards. The gallery illustrates ways of life and systems of belief very different from those valued by Western cultures. These values are as much the subject of the gallery as are the sculptures, bronzes and ceramics produced by the different societies, which have inhabited this large area.

The South Asia section uses objects to chart the major religious systems developed in India: Buddhism, Hinduism and Jainism. It also examines the impact of these religious systems on Thailand and Cambodia.

The other half of the gallery traces Chinese civilisation chronologically. A common written language binds the vast country together and links the present with the past. Some modern characters remain the same as those written nearly 4000 years ago.

Bodhisattva Tara
Tara is a popular Buddhist goddess, the consort of Avalokiteshvara, the *bodhisattva* of compassion. This bronze statue was found on the east coast of Sri Lanka, and is evidence of the presence in the medieval period of Mahayana Buddhism, which is generally more associatated with the north of India.
Found between Trincomalee and Batticaloa, Sri Lanka, made AD 700–750. H 1.43 m

Figure of Shiva Nataraja

The Hindu god Shiva appears here as the Lord of the Dance, Nataraja, in a ring of fire. Nestling within his hair is a small figure, the goddess Ganga, the personification of the holy River Ganges. The Nataraja is one of the best known images in Indian art and many are placed in temple shrines and paraded during festivals.

From Tamil Nadu, southern India, around AD 1100. H 89 cm

Jar depicting a dragon

The Chinese perfected the *cloisonné* enamel technique, used to make this jar and domed cover, in the AD 1400s. By the time this jar was made it was considered appropriate for the emperor's use. Many superb pieces were made for palaces and temples. The inscription on the neck shows it was made for the Imperial Household.

From China, AD 1426–1435. H 62 cm

Asia
India: Amaravati

The Asahi Shimbun Gallery of Amaravati Sculpture
Room 33a
Ground floor, Level 1
300 BC–AD 400

Amaravati in south-east India, was one of the most important Buddhist sites in India. It was founded in 300–200 BC and was in continual use for more than 1000 years. The Amaravati sculptures consist of carved relief panels showing narrative scenes from the life of the Buddha, as well as Buddhist emblems and symbols. They were used to decorate the outside of a stūpa, a large dome-shaped mound that once contained Buddhist relics and votive offerings.

Pair of *Buddhapada*
In the early period of Buddhist sculpture in India, the Buddha was not represented in human form. Instead he was depicted through symbols. This limestone panel depicts the *Buddhapada,* the Buddha's footprints.
From the Great Stūpa at Amaravati, Guntur District, Andhra Pradesh, India, 100–1 BC. H 67 cm

The Great Stūpa
This limestone drum slab is carved with a scene of the Great Stūpa itself. It helps us to reconstruct what the Great Stūpa would have looked like and where the reliefs that survive would originally have been placed.
From the Great Stūpa at Amaravati, Guntur District, Andhra Pradesh, India, 100 BC–AD 200s. H 1.24 m

Asia
Chinese jade

The Selwyn and Ellie Alleyne Gallery
Room 33b
Ground floor, Level 1
About 5000 BC–present

In China, jade has been highly valued for thousands of years, and revered as a rare and precious material associated with power and wealth. The objects on display in this room illustrate the history of the precious stone, prized for its beauty and magical properties. Translucent yet tough, jade was worked into ornaments, ceremonial weapons and ritual objects by Chinese craftspeople.

Jade headdress ornament
A powerful coiled dragon emerges from the top of this headdress ornament. This type of ornament was worn on the top of hats as seen in portraits of Mongol aristocrats. Such ornaments were still popular in the early Ming dynasty.
China, AD 1300s–1400s. H 6 cm

Asia
Korea

The Korea Foundation Gallery
Room 67
Ground floor, Level 2
300 BC–present

The distinct culture of Korea developed from a wealth of native tradition combined with interactions with neighbouring civilisations. Sitting at a crossroads, the location of the Korean peninsula played a crucial role not only in establishing its diverse cultural heritage, but also in the development of East Asian culture and art. Since 1948 the peninsula has been divided into the Republic of Korea in the south and the Democratic People's Republic of Korea in the north.

Objects on display date from about 300 BC to the present and include ceramics, metalwork, sculpture, prints, calligrapy and painting. The reconstruction of a *saranbang*, or scholar's study, reflects the importance of traditional architecture, which continues to be held in high esteem today.

Moon jar

This white porcelain jar is a magnificent example of the ceramic art of the Joseon period (AD 1392–1910). At this time, plain white porcelain represented the epitome of austerity, frugality and purity, principles favoured by Confucianism, the dominant ideology of the period.

From Korea, AD 1650–1750. H 47 cm

Guardian King of the North

This large painting on hemp cloth, one of a pair, is from late in the Joseon period, when Buddhism became more active after a time of repression. The size of the canvas, the dynamic and decorative lines, and the combination of mineral colours are typical of Buddhist paintings from this period.

From Korea, AD 1796–1820. H 3 m

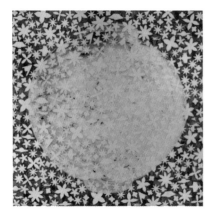

Samramansang Moon Jar #1 (2010–2013)

This mixed media work by Kang Ik-joong (b. 1960) consists of 225 squares covered with an image of a moon jar, an iconic type of Korean porcelain, and a layer of white flowers mixed with images of fighter jets and attack helicopters. The background of the squares each contain an image of a seated Buddha.

Made in New York, USA. H 1.14 m

Celadon bowl

This bowl exemplifies an underglaze inlay technique innovated during the Goryeo period (AD 918–1392). Potters filled the crevices of the incised motifs with clay slip before glazing, which creates the lovely white and black images of the willows, reeds, and ducks. The two characters in the centre indicate a date of AD 1329.

From Korea, AD 1329. Diam. 26 cm

Asia
Painting and calligraphy

Room 91a
Upper floors, Level 4
500 AD–present

This room is dedicated to the display of painting and calligraphy from China. The changing display includes early Buddhist paintings and modern works of calligraphy. Due to its fragility and for conservation reasons, the Admonitions Scroll is only on display for six-week periods. When not on display you will be able to see a digital version of the scroll on an interactive touchscreen.

The Admonitions Scroll
The Admonitions of the Instructress to the Court Ladies is one of the most important Chinese paintings to survive anywhere in the world. It is traditionally attributed to Gu Kaizhi (about AD 344–406) and is an early example of the combination of the three arts: poetry, calligraphy and painting.
From China, AD 500s–700s.
L 3.43 m

出其言善千里應之苟違斯義
同衾以疑

Asia
Japan

The Mitsubishi Corporation Japanese Galleries
Rooms 92–94
Upper floors, Level 5
5000 BC–present

Japan has become a thriving modern, high-tech society while continuing to celebrate many elements of its traditional culture. These rooms explore how continuity and change have shaped Japan's past and present, and its relationship with the rest of the world. The galleries focus on a series of themes, from ancient Japan (13,500 BC–AD 1200), to medieval Japan (AD 1200–AD 1600), through the Edo period (AD 1600–1868), to modern Japan (AD 1853 to the present).

The art, religion, entertainment and everyday life of emperors, courtiers and townspeople are illustrated through a remarkable range of objects from porcelain and Samurai warrior swords, to woodblock prints and 20th-century manga comic books. Historic tea ceremony wares can also be seen, alongside a reconstruction of a traditional tea house.

Statue of Fudō Myō-ō
Fudō Myō-ō is an important deity in Tantric Buddhism. His name, 'immovable', reflects the unchanging nature of reality beneath the illusion of his fierce exterior. He is one of the 'Kings of Light', a constant enemy of illusion, pointing the way to enlightenment.
From Japan, AD 1100s. H 89 cm

Samurai armour and helmet
This suit of armour brings together different pieces made between AD 1500 and 1800. With the arrival of guns with the Portugese in the AD 1500s, thick bullet-proof metal breast plates were added to armour. Samurai rulers used the threat of military action to keep Japan at peace.
From Japan, late AD 1500s–1800s. H 1.25 m

Young woman mask for Nō drama
Nō performances were developed in the AD 1300–1400s. There are a number of different masks that are used in different dramas and the mask is treated as containing a spirit of its own. A skilfully carved mask such as this one will appear to have subtle changes of expression depending on the way in which the wearer turns their head.
From Japan, AD 1700s–1800s. H 21 cm

Kakiemon elephant
During the Edo period (AD 1600–1868), models of animals were made for European mantlepieces. Real elephants would not have been seen in Japan at this time and this unusual example, based on a South Asian animal, was probably ordered by merchants of the Dutch East India Company for export. The Kakiemon style, creamy body and enamel colouring, was desirable and expensive, sought after by wealthy European collectors.
From Japan, late AD 1600s. H 35 cm

Asia
Chinese ceramics – Sir Percival David Collection

The Sir Joseph Hotung Centre for Ceramic Studies
Room 95
Ground floor, Level 2
AD 200s–AD 1900s

Porcelain was first produced in China around AD 600. The skilful transformation of ordinary clay into beautiful objects has captivated the imagination of people throughout history and across the globe. Chinese ceramics, by far the most advanced in the world, were made for the imperial court, the domestic market or for export.

Within this gallery of almost 1700 objects are examples of the finest Chinese ceramics in the world, dating from the AD 200s–1900s. Some are unique creations, while others were mass-produced in batches of several hundred at a time. Technological innovations and the use of regional raw materials mean that Chinese ceramics are visually diverse.

Vase with butterflies and daylilies
The Yongle Emperor, (r. 1403–1424) was the third Ming dynasty ruler and the commissions he made for his court revolutionised the technical qualities of porcelain at Jingdezhen, introducing new patterns and a higher firing body. Wine bottles such as this would have been taken as diplomatic gifts to various courts in Southeast Asia, the Middle East and the east coast of Africa as well as being provided for the imperial court at Beijing.
From Jingdezhen, China,
AD 1403–1425. H 34 cm

Moon-shaped flask with birds

The design on this flask is centuries old but its decoration in terms of colours and technical skill is an innovation made during the Qing dynasty, Yongzheng period (AD 1723–1735).

From Jingdezhen, China, AD 1723–1735. H 29 cm

The David Vases

These vases are among the most important examples of blue-and-white porcelain in existence, and are probably the best-known porcelain vases in the world. They were made for the altar of a Daoist temple and they are important because their inscription dates them to a specific time.

From Jingdezhen, China, AD 1351. H 63 cm

Pear-shaped covered ewer

The shape of this ewer is modelled on a metal prototype, probably silverware, but possibly bronze. Its detailing, such as the base of the handle which splits into three perfectly formed sections, is very fine.

From Longquan region, China, about AD 1300–1368. H 21 cm

Europe

The European collection covers the cultures and long history of Britain and other parts of Europe. It includes some of the best-known prehistoric and Roman material found in Britain, reflecting aspects of life in these islands from the time of the hunter-gatherers to that of the Roman province of Britannia.

Objects featured in the displays include a 10,000-year-old antler headdress, mysterious stone balls carved by northern craftsmen, warrior gear and luxury items of bronze and precious metal, and hoards of gold and silver jewellery and plate.

The collection continues chronologically through medieval, Renaissance and modern Europe. Objects on display include the Sutton Hoo ship burial and the Lewis Chessmen.

Europe
Medieval Europe AD 1050–1500

The Sir Paul and Lady Ruddock Gallery of Medieval Europe
Room 40
Upper floors, Level 3

This room showcases many of the Museum's greatest medieval treasures. British and European objects tell the story of a period of great change when territorial wars and political turmoil began to shape the continent we know today.

From the power and dominance of the Church in everyday life, to the social change spread through Europe by a new merchant class, unique and famous objects provide a gateway to the major developments of the age. The ritual and protocol of the royal court is explored, as well as the cultural, intellectual and political exchange brought about by travel, trade and pilgrimage. Examples of sacred art also show how the divine was represented at the time.

The Lewis Chessmen
These chess pieces, found on the Isle of Lewis, Scotland, consist of elaborately worked walrus ivory and whales' teeth in the forms of seated kings and queens, mitred bishops, knights on their mounts, standing rooks and pawns in the shape of obelisks.
Probably made in Scandinavia, thought to be Norway, about AD 1150–1200. H 4 cm–10 cm

Icon of the Triumph of Orthodoxy

This Christian icon, a devotional image from the Orthodox tradition, is itself a picture of another icon. It celebrates the end of a period in Orthodox Christianity when the use of icons and other religious images were banned and destroyed.

From Constantinople (modern Istanbul), about 1400. H 39 cm

Parade shield

A knight declaring his love, or taking leave from a lady, was a popular theme in medieval and Renaissance courtly art. Although constructed like a battle shield, it was not used for protection, and was probably only used during parades and other courtly festivals.

From Flanders or Burgundy, Belgium or France, late AD 1400s. H 83 cm

Citole

A citole is the medieval equivalent of a guitar. This is the only surviving example from the time and is an outstanding example of medieval secular art, carved with intricate woodland scenes, real and imaginary.

From England, about AD 1280–1330. L 61 cm

The Royal Gold Cup

This cup is made of solid gold and is lavishly decorated with translucent enamels. It depicts scenes from the life, miracles and martyrdom of St Agnes. The band of Tudor roses on the cup's stem were inserted under Henry VIII when the cup was in the English royal treasury.

From Paris, France, about AD 1370–1380. H 24 cm

Europe
Sutton Hoo and Europe AD 300–1100

The Sir Paul and Lady Ruddock Gallery of Sutton Hoo and Europe
Room 41
Upper floors, Level 3

The centuries AD 300–1100 witnessed great change
in Europe. The Roman Empire disintegrated in
the west, but continued in the east as the Byzantine
Empire until AD 1453. People, objects and ideas
travelled across the continent and its seas, while
Christianity and Islam emerged as major religions.
By AD 1100 the precursors of several modern states
had developed. Europe as we know it today was
beginning to take shape.

This room gives an overview of the period and its
peoples, and traces the developments through objects
from everyday items to church treasures. The gallery's
centrepiece is the Anglo-Saxon ship burial at Sutton
Hoo, Suffolk – one of the most spectacular and
important discoveries in British archaeology.

Gold belt-buckle
The Sutton Hoo ship burial is an astonishing
20th-century discovery from an Anglo-Saxon
royal cemetery, which included Byzantine
and other treasures.
From Sutton Hoo, Suffolk, England,
early AD 600s. L 13 cm

The Franks Casket

The carvings on this magnificent whalebone casket tell stories from Germanic legends, Christianity and the Classical world. It is inscribed with Anglo-Saxon runic letters and Latin.

Probably made in Northumbria, England, about AD 700. H 11 cm

The Sutton Hoo Helmet

This extraordinary helmet is very rare and one of only four known complete helmets from Anglo-Saxon England. It was badly damaged when the burial chamber collapsed, but conservators have managed to reconstruct the helmet. A complete replica, also on display, shows how the original would have looked.

From Sutton Hoo, Suffolk, England, early AD 600s. H 32 cm

The Lycurgus Cup

This extraordinary cup is the only complete example of a very special type of glass, known as dichroic, which changes colour when held up to the light. The opaque green cup turns to a glowing translucent red when light is shone through it.

Probably made in Rome, AD 300s. H 16 cm

Europe
Europe 1400–1800

The period dating from the late Middle Ages until the end of the 18th century was a time of great social change in Europe. Religious conflict, civil war and revolution challenged both individual and national identities and the discovery of new continents radically reshaped the European world view.

This room charts the expansion of international trade, the growth of modern cities and the major developments in the arts and sciences that established the broad outline of modern European civilisation.

Bust of Oliver Cromwell by Roubillac
A Member of Parliament at the outbreak of the English Civil War in 1642, Cromwell soon established a formidable military reputation and was installed as Lord Protector in 1653. After the Restoration of Charles II to the throne, his body was exhumed from Westminster Abbey and his head was set on a pole on top of Westminster Hall.
From London, England, about AD 1759. H 63 cm

Medal of Mary I by Jacopo da Trezzo
This medal depicting Queen Mary I of England (r. 1553–1558) is by a Milanese artist. Almost certainly commissioned by Mary's husband, Philip II of Spain, it presents her as a member of the imperial Hapsburg family and a restorer of peace.
From London, AD 1554. Diam. 69 mm

The Medici Vase
The Islamic tradition of lustred earthenware was introduced into Europe in the workshops of Malaga, in Islamic southern Spain. However, by around 1400 the Christian regime of Valencia had become the major centre of production.
From Valencia, Spain, AD 1465–1492. H 57 cm

Maiolica plate
This tin-glazed maiolica plate shows soldiers, who have been bathing, responding to the call to battle. The scene is based on a print after a design by Michelangelo showing an episode from Florentine history, *The Battle of Cascina* in 1364. The plate was made as a display piece for the scholar Cardinal Pietro Bembo, as shown by his coat of arms.
From Urbino, Italy, AD 1539–1547. Diam. 27 cm

Europe
Europe 1800–1900

Room 47
Upper floors, Level 3

The 1800s saw unprecedented economic growth in Europe, accompanied by immense social and political upheavals. For Britain it was a period of stability and industrial supremacy. On the continent, France underwent three revolutions, while the second half of the century saw the unification of Germany and of Italy.

The nationalist sentiment that lay behind these events often paid homage to the great ages of the past. This is reflected in the objects on display, many of which have borrowed motifs from earlier historical periods.

The Pegasus Vase
This vase is made of jasper ware, a type of unglazed stoneware that can be stained with colour before firing. Josiah Wedgewood (1730–1795) perfected the technique by 1775, after a number of experiments. The main scene shows the Apotheosis of Homer, copied from a Greek vase bought by the Museum in 1763.
Made in the Etruria factory, Staffordshire, England, about AD 1786. H 46 cm

Teapot designed by Christopher Dresser
Christopher Dresser (1834–1904) sought to take advantage of the opportunity presented by industry to make good design available at a cheaper price. His success required experiments along the way: this unique electroplate teapot was made by hand from sheet metal and was too expensive to put into production.
Made in Sheffield, England, AD 1879–1885. H 18 cm

Europe
Europe 1900 to the present

Room 48
Upper floors, Level 3

The 1900s saw greater changes than any previous century, from air travel to fully automated production processes. The upheavals of two world wars led to widespread movement of peoples. Many Europeans emigrated to North America, while innovations in American lifestyle had a profound influence in Europe. Despite increasing globalisation, many countries maintained a sense of national identity.

This room shows changing displays and is continuously updated as new objects are acquired.

Russian revolutionary plate
After the Russian Revolution of October 1917, factories were nationalised and artists created designs for ceramics, textiles and posters disseminating the messages of the new Soviet Republic. This plate is inscribed with a slogan urging the virtue of learning: 'Knowledge in your head means grain on the threshing floor', with a pile of books, pen and paper on top of the Soviet symbols of hammer and sickle. *From St Petersburg, Russia, AD 1920, Diam. 22 cm*

Europe
Roman Britain

The Weston Gallery
Room 49
Upper floors, Level 3
AD 43–about AD 411

The Roman emperor Claudius invaded Britain in AD 43. By AD 100, England and Wales and some of Scotland had been conquered. The Romans built towns, roads and villas. Latin became the official language and Roman law and coinage were introduced. Imported goods and settlers from Europe, the Middle East and North Africa created a richer, more diverse society and a wealth of mosaics, wall paintings, sculpture, glassware, pottery and metalwork were produced.

The laws, administration, currency, architecture, engineering, religion and art of Rome met Britain's Iron Age societies to create a distinctive 'Romano-British' identity, which is illustrated through a variety of objects and artworks. The province collapsed in the early 5th century as continental peoples from beyond the frontiers invaded.

The Mildenhall Great Dish
The most famous object in the Mildenhall treasure is the large, highly decorated circular platter. The subject matter alludes to the worship and mythology of Bacchus, the god of wine. Bacchic imagery had a long history in Greek and Roman art and this is one of the finest examples to survive from the late-Roman period.
Found near Mildenhall, Suffolk, Roman Britain, made AD 300s. Diam. 60 cm

Hinton St Mary mosaic (detail)

This magnificent mosaic was discovered buried beneath a field in the village of Hinton St Mary, Dorset, in 1963. In the central roundel is what is thought to be one of the earliest representations of Christ, and, if so, is the only such portrait on a mosaic floor from anywhere in the Roman Empire.

From Dorset, Roman Britain, AD 300s. L 8.1 m (roundel diam. 83 cm)

Tomb of Classicianus

This is the reconstructed tomb of Gaius Julius Alpinus Classicianus. He was the finance minister of Britain after the revolt of the Iceni led by Queen Boudica in AD 60–61. His job was to correct the financial abuses that had been an important cause of the rebellion.

From Trinity Square, London, Roman Britain, AD 60s. H 2.18 m

The emperor Hadrian

Hadrian (r. AD 117–138) is the emperor who built the 80-mile-long wall across Britain 'to separate the barbarians from the Romans'. This head comes from a statue that probably stood in Roman London in a public space such as a forum.

Found in the River Thames, near London Bridge, Roman Britain, made AD 100s. H 43 cm

Europe
Britain and Europe 800 BC–AD 43
Room 50
Upper floors, Level 3

The Iron Age was a time of change for people across Europe. Although metalsmiths continued to use bronze, gold and other metals, they also learned to work with iron, which improved farming technologies and created new relationships between communities. Most people lived on farms or in small villages, but in some areas there were now larger settlements and hillforts.

From around 500 BC, Greek authors wrote of peoples called 'Keltoi' living in Europe north of the Alps. Although archaeology suggests many distinct groups rather than a single people, they shared a unique abstract art style that we now call Celtic art.

Basse-Yutz Flagon
Used for serving wine, ale or mead at feasts, these flagons from eastern France are among the finest examples of early Celtic art. They copy the shape of bronze flagons made and used by the Etruscans in northern Italy. But the metalsmith has imaginatively incorporated stylised Celtic designs, such as the staring faces at the bases of the handles.
From Basse-Yutz, Lorraine, France, 420–360 BC. H 40 cm

The Great Torc
One of the most elaborate golden objects from the ancient world, this torc is made from just over a kilogram of gold and silver. The neck ring is formed of 64 wires, twisted in sets of 8, finished with strikingly decorated cast terminals. It was buried as part of a hoard, probably as an offering to the gods.
Found at Ken Hill, Snettisham, Norfolk, England, made about 75 BC. Diam. 20 cm

Europe
Europe and Middle East 10,000–800 BC

Room 51
Upper floors, Level 3

Farming began in the Middle East around 12,000 years ago, making possible the social, cultural and economic changes which shaped the modern world. Europe was similarly transformed as early farmers gradually spread into new areas, eventually reaching Britain 6000 years ago.

The objects on display show how the people of prehistoric Europe engaged with the natural and spirit worlds, making use of the resources at their disposal. The introduction of metal from mainland Europe to Britain around 2500 BC saw important developments in social and economical relationships.

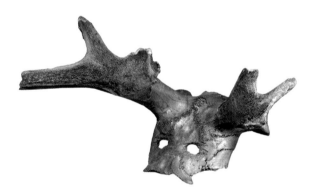

Gold cape
Workmen quarrying for stone in an ancient burial mound in 1833 found this unique ceremonial gold cape, which remains unparalleled to this day. The cape would have been unsuitable for everyday wear because it would have severely restricted upper arm movement. Instead it would have served ceremonial roles, and may have denoted religious authority.
From Mold, Flintshire, North Wales, about 1900–1600 BC. H 23 cm

Red deer antler headdress
This headdress may have been worn by hunters as a disguise, but it is more likely to have been part of a costume worn on special occasions, perhaps during religious ceremonies.
From Star Carr, Vale of Pickering, North Yorkshire, England, about 8000 BC. H 15 cm

Middle East

This collection covers the ancient and contemporary civilisations and cultures of the Middle East from the Neolithic period until the present. There is a wide range of archaeological material and ancient art from Mesopotamia (Iraq), Iran, the Levant (Syria, Jordan, Lebanon and Israel), Anatolia (Turkey), Arabia, Central Asia and the Caucasus. Highlights of the collection include Assyrian reliefs, treasure from the Royal Cemetery of Ur, the Oxus Treasure, Phoenician ivories and King Ashurbanipal's library of cuneiform tablets from Nineveh in northern Iraq.

At its peak, the Neo-Assyrian Empire stretched from Cyprus in the Mediterranean to the Persian Gulf and from the Caucasus Mountains (Armenia, Georgia, Azerbaijan) to the Arabian Peninsula and Egypt. Between 934–609 BC the Neo-Assyrian Empire was the most powerful state on earth.

The Islamic collection includes archaeological assemblages from Iraq, Iran and Egypt as well as inlaid metalwork from medieval Iran, Syria and Egypt, and Iznik ceramics from Turkey. In addition to Persian, Turkish and Mughal Indian works on paper, the Museum holds a major collection of contemporary art from the Middle East.

Middle East
Assyrian sculpture and Balawat Gates

Monumental stone sculptures and reliefs were a striking feature of many of the palaces and temples of ancient Assyria (modern northern Iraq). Sculptures on display include two colossal winged human-headed lions from an entrance to the throne room of King Ashurnasirpal II (r. 883–859 BC) at Nimrud and a gigantic standing lion from the temple of Ishtar Sharrat-niphi.

The Black Obelisk of Shalmaneser III
This stone obelisk glorifies the achievements of King Shalmaneser III (r. 858–824 BC) and his commander in chief. It lists their military campaigns and is notable for showing the submission, among others, of Jehu of Israel. It also illustrates some of the tribute exacted from Assyria's neighbours: including exotic camels, monkeys, an elephant and a rhinoceros. Assyrian kings often collected rare animals and plants as an expression of their power and dominion. *From Nimrud (ancient Kalhu), northern Iraq, 858–824 BC. H 1.98 m*

Statue of a human-headed winged lion
Supernatural stone mythological guardians, sculpted in relief or in the round, were often placed at gateways to ancient Mesopotamian palaces to protect them from demonic forces. *From Nimrud (ancient Kalhu), northern Iraq, about 883–859 BC*

Middle East
Assyria: Nimrud

Rooms 7–8
Ground floor, Level 0
883–859 BC

The Neo-Assyrian king Ashurnasirpal II (883–859 BC) built the magnificent North-West Palace at his new capital of Nimrud (now in northern Iraq). Its interior decoration featured a series of remarkable carved stone wall panels, the first known from Assyria.

Most reliefs in the palace were of protective supernatural figures, and the narrative reliefs mainly stood in the throne room. Here, to celebrate his achievements, Ashurnasirpal is shown defeating his enemies, receiving tribute, and hunting wild bulls and lions.

Relief from the North-West Palace of Ashurnasirpal II
Reliefs were originally set against the brick interior walls of the palace and would have been brightly painted. This gypsum panel from the throne room shows the king hunting from a chariot. Royal lion hunts, sometimes with a ritual purpose, were a very old tradition in Mesopotamia, with examples known in art as early as 3000 BC.
From Nimrud (ancient Kalhu), northern Iraq, 883–859 BC, L 2.23 m

Panel of Ashurnasirpal II with tribute bearers
This gypsum relief panel comes from the walls of the courtyard which led to the throne room of the king. It shows foreigners, probably Phoenicians from the Levant, bringing exotic monkeys as part of their tribute.
From Nimrud (ancient Kalhu), northern Iraq, 883–859 BC. H 2.63 m

Middle East
Assyria: Nineveh

Room 9
Ground floor, Level 0
700–692 BC

The rooms and courtyards of the Neo-Assyrian South-West Palace of King Sennacherib (r. 704–681 BC) at Nineveh (in northern Iraq) were decorated with a large number of finely carved stone panels.

The panels depicted a variety of highly animated scenes, including the construction of the palace, with the transport of huge sculptures of human-headed winged bulls that can weigh up to 30 tons. These illustrations provide an insight into ancient quarrying and transport techniques, as well as Sennacherib's keen interest in his spectacular building projects. Other panels on display here were re-carved by Sennacherib's grandson, Ashurbanipal, and show his military campaigns in Babylonia (southern Iraq).

Stone panel from the South-West Palace of Sennacherib (detail)
Instead of the usual scenes of warfare, hunting or the receipt of tribute shown on relief panels, this shows the transport of an unfinished human-headed winged bull from a quarry. The colossal sculpture is being levered forward onto a sledge to be hauled to the new palace at Nineveh while other materials go by boat.
From Nineveh, northern Iraq, about 700–681 BC

Middle East
Assyria: Lion hunts, siege of Lachish and Khorsabad

Room 10
Ground floor, Level 0
645–705 BC

The sculpted reliefs illustrate the hunting exploits of the last great Assyrian king, Ashurbanipal (r. 668–631/630 BC) and the capture in 701 BC of the city of Lachish in the southern Levant by the Assyrian king, Sennacherib. The campaign followed the refusal of King Hezekiah of Judah to pay tribute to the Assyrian Empire and is mentioned in the Bible.

Reliefs and statues from the city and palace of King Sargon II at Khorsabad (in northern Iraq) are also on display. The palace entrances were originally dominated by pairs of colossal human-headed winged bulls, which were intended as supernatural guardians, accompanied by protective spirits with magical powers.

Stone panel from the North Palace of Ashurbanipal
This finely carved gypsum wall panel shows closely observed studies of some of the exotic plants and animals, in this case lions, kept in Assyrian royal parks and gardens, essentially as specimens and trophies.
From Nineveh, northern Iraq, 645 BC. H 98 cm

Middle East
Islamic world

The John Addis Islamic Gallery
Room 34
Ground floor, Level -1
AD 700–present

The objects in this gallery date from around AD 700 to the present day. They reveal the breadth and richness of Islamic culture from Spain to China.

The first part of the gallery introduces the faith of Islam and art from the early Islamic era. It highlights the importance of calligraphy, science and cross-cultural links beyond the Middle East. The lower level provides a geographical and chronological coverage of the history and art of the Islamic lands. A changing display is dedicated to works on paper.

The term 'Islamic' is used here to define the culture of peoples living in lands where the dominant religion is (or was) Islam. The term applies to religious works of art as well as objects of everyday use.

Jade terrapin
This life-sized terrapin is carved from a single piece of jade and was found in Allahabad, India. It was probably made to be an ornament for the garden of a Mughal palace.
From Allahabad, India, AD 1600–1605. H 20 cm

The Blacas Ewer

This ewer is a masterful example of medieval Islamic inlaid brass. Mosul metalworkers inlaid brass vessels with intricate courtly scenes in silver and copper to create glittering objects. They were often given as diplomatic gifts to neighbouring rulers.
From Mosul, northern Iraq, AD 1232. H 30 cm

Enamelled glass canteen

This was certainly a luxury object, perhaps made specifically as a gift. The decorations include horsemen similar to iconography found in Christian art, and medallions depicting musicians, typical of figures found in Islamic art. The mixture of motifs suggests the patron was either a Muslim who was familiar with Christian imagery, or a Christian who appreciated the work of Muslim craftsmen.
From Syria, AD 1330–1350. H 23 cm

Footed basin

This large basin may have been used for washing the feet of Sultan Süleyman II (r. AD 1520–1566). The basin is an example of the 'Damascus' style of Iznik pottery. Distinctive elements of the decoration, such as the cloud scrolls, show stylistic links with an Iznik mosque lamp, also in the Museum's collection, which provides a useful basis for attributing date and location of origin to the basin.
From Iznik (modern Turkey), about AD 1545–1550. H 27 cm

Peacock and stand

This steel peacock may have decorated the cross-bar of an *alam*, a standard carried during religious festivals in Iran. Peacocks were symbols of beauty and the pleasures of the court throughout the Islamic world.
From Iran, AD 1800s. H 89 cm

Middle East
Ancient Iran

The Rahim Irvani Gallery
Room 52
Upper floors, Level 3
3000 BC–AD 651

Iran was a major centre of ancient culture. It was rich in valuable natural resources, especially metals, and played an important role in the development of ancient Middle Eastern civilisation and trade.

The objects on display demonstrate the strength of its local crafts and the close trade contacts it enjoyed with neighbouring regions. The 19th-century casts around the walls and on the east stairs are of reliefs from the ancient Persian capital of Persepolis.

During the 6th century BC, Cyrus the Great founded a Persian empire, which eventually stretched from Egypt to Pakistan. Objects on display from this period include the Cyrus Cylinder and the Oxus Treasure. The later periods of the Parthian and Sasanian empires mark a revival in Iranian culture and are represented through displays including silver plates and cut glass.

**Griffin-headed armlet
from the Oxus Treasure**
The Oxus Treasure is the most important collection of gold and silver to have survived from the Achaemenid period (550–331 BC). Armlets were among the items considered as gifts of honour at the Persian court. The hollow spaces would have contained inlays of glass or semi-precious stones.
From the region of Takht-I Kuwad, Tajikistan, 500–300 BC. H 12 cm

The Cyrus Cylinder

This fired clay document is inscribed in Babylonian cuneiform with an account by Cyrus, ruler of Iran (559–530 BC), of his peaceful capture of the Neo-Babylonian capital of Babylon in 539 BC. He also presents himself as a worshipper of the Babylonian chief god Marduk and Cyrus claims to have restored the temples and religious cults, and to have returned their previously deported gods and people.

From Babylon, southern Iraq, about 539–530 BC. L 22 cm

Relief of a winged male sphinx

This sphinx wears the imposing horned headdress of a divinity. It was originally painted and was set up on a façade of a palace before being transferred to the staircase of another palace in Persepolis.

From Palace H at Persepolis, south-west Iran, 500–400 BC. H 82 cm

Silver plate

The Sasanian empire stretched from the River Euphrates to the River Indus and included modern-day Armenia and Georgia. This gilded silver dish is typical of the high-quality silverware produced during the Sasanian empire. It shows Shapur II (r. AD 309–379) – who restored the Sasanian empire after a short period during which much territory was lost – on a lion hunt.

Sasanian, AD 300s. Diam. 18 cm

Middle East
Ancient South Arabia

The Raymond and Beverly Sackler Wing
Room 53
Upper floors, Level 3

Ancient South Arabia was centred on what is now modern Yemen, but included parts of Saudi Arabia and southern Oman. It was famous in the ancient world as an important source of valuable incense and perfume, and was described by Classical writers as Arabia Felix ('Fortunate Arabia') because of its fertility.

Several important kingdoms flourished there at different times between 1000 BC and the rise of Islam in the 6th century AD. The oldest and most important of these was Saba, which is referred to as Sheba in the Bible.

Tin-bronze altar with a Sabaean dedication
The people of ancient South Arabia worshipped a variety of gods and goddesses, built large temples for the main gods and made offerings to them in shrines. This altar, with an inscription in Sabaean, is dedicated to a local deity, Ramhaw.
From Marib, Yemen, 100 BC– AD 100. H 1.1 m

Incense burner
In Arabia, camels were domesticated and camel caravan transported aromatics to market across the region. This incense burner is inscribed in Sabaean, one of the several related Semitic languages spoken in ancient South Arabia. It was written using an alphabet that changed little between its origins in the 6th century BC and its disappearance in the 7th century AD.
From Shabwa, Yemen, 300–200 BC. H 32 cm

Middle East
Anatolia and Urartu 7000–300 BC

The Raymond and Beverly Sackler Wing
Room 54
Upper floors, Level 3

Ancient Anatolia and Urartu form an important land link between Europe and Asia and lie where the modern Republic of Turkey, Armenia, Georgia and north-west Iran are located today. Objects on display represent different cultures from prehistoric to Hellenistic times and illustrate trade between different regions alongside examples of Bronze Age and Iron Age craftsmanship.

Relief showing a storm-god
This is a fragment of a basalt relief depicting the Syrian storm-god, identified by his knobbed horned headdress, long curl of hair and by the axe he is brandishing. It comes from the so-called 'Herald's Wall' opposite the temple of the storm-god at Carchemish.
From Carchemish, south-east Anatolia (modern Turkey), 1000–900 BC. H 58 cm

Silver bull
This is an example of Early Bronze Age craftsmanship. It may have come from the top of a pole supporting a canopy over a rich burial. It is very similar to those found with jewellery and daggers in princely graves at Alaca Hüyük, which may have been the centre of an influential and wealthy merchant kingdom.
Probably from Alaca Hüyük (modern Turkey), around 2350 BC. H 24 cm

Middle East
Mesopotamia 1500–539 BC

The Raymond and Beverly Sackler Wing
Room 55
Upper floors, Level 3

Between 1500 and 500 BC the area of modern Iraq and north-eastern Syria shared a common culture, but was divided between the northern kingdom of Assyria and the southern kingdom of Babylonia. The expansion of both these powers led in turn to the incorporation of much of the Middle East into a single empire, which was eventually taken over by the Persian King Cyrus in 539 BC.

This room shows both the military might of the Assyrian army and the importance of literature within their culture. King Ashurbanipal (r. 668–631/630 BC) collected cuneiform clay tablets to create the first library in the world to contain all knowledge. The room also charts the rise of the city of Babylon under King Nebuchadnezzar II and his building programme, which created the city's famous walls, ziggurat, temples and gardens. Texts on clay tablets also describe events and people known from the Bible and the fall of the Babylonian Empire under King Nabonidus and his Regent Belshazzar.

Map of the World
This tablet is a unique map of the Mesopotamian world. Babylon is shown in the centre, and Assyria, Elam and other places are also named. The cuneiform inscription records traditions from much earlier times, and even refers to where the Babylonian Ark landed.
Probably from Sippar, southern Iraq, 700–500 BC. H 12 cm

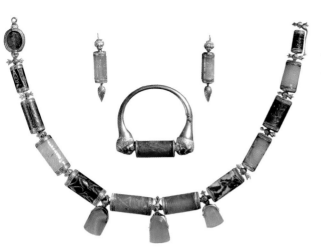

Lady Layard's Necklace

This necklace was part of a set made as a wedding present from Sir Austen Henry Layard to his bride Enid. It was created from ancient cylinder seals and stamp-seals acquired by him during his travels and excavations in the Middle East.

Stone seals from Iraq, 2200–350 BC; gold setting made in London, mid AD 1800s.

The Flood Tablet

This is the most famous cuneiform tablet in the world. It relates part of the Epic of Gilgamesh, the story of a ruler of Uruk and his search for immortality. The cuneiform text is startlingly similar to the biblical story of Noah and his Ark in the Book of Genesis and describes how the gods sent a flood to destroy mankind.

From Nineveh, northern Iraq, 700–600 BC. L 15 cm

Brick panel showing a roaring lion

Glazed bricks in bright shades of blue, yellow and white were used to depict mythical and real animals symbolising the king and the gods. Roaring lions represented King Nebuchadnezzar II himself.

From Babylon, southern Iraq, 605–562 BC.

Middle East
Mesopotamia 6000–1500 BC

The Raymond and Beverly Sackler Wing
Room 56
Upper floors, Level 3

Between 6000 and 1500 BC, Mesopotamia, the land between the Tigris and Euphrates rivers (now Iraq, north-east Syria and part of south-east Turkey) witnessed momentous advances in the development of human civilisation.

The objects on display span the transition from small agricultural villages to the world's first cities and empires. They illustrate the important aspects of daily life in early cities, such as literacy and bureaucracy, religion and ritual, warfare and diplomacy, music and banqueting, and preparation for the afterlife.

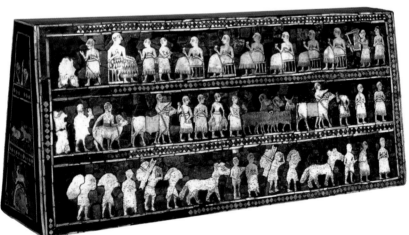

The Standard of Ur
This unusual object with vivid scenes of war and feasting was found in one of the largest graves in the Royal Cemetery at Ur (modern Iraq), lying in the corner of a chamber above the right shoulder of a man. While its original function is not yet understood, the inlaid panels depict two complementary aspects of Sumerian kingship: the ruler as a warrior and the ruler as a provider of peace and prosperity.
From Ur, southern Iraq, about 2600–2400 BC. L 49 cm

Ram in a Thicket

This gilded wooden figure was found in the 'Great Death Pit' at the Royal Cemetery of Ur, which held the multiple remains of elaborately dressed individuals, who may have been court musicians and entertainers. The Ram was originally part of a support for some form of stand or musical instrument. It is beautifully crafted using precious imported materials such as gold, copper and lapis lazuli.
From Ur, southern Iraq, about 2600–2400 BC. H 46 cm

The Queen of the Night

This baked clay plaque depicts a winged Mesopotamian goddess standing on the backs of two lions. The goddess was originally painted red while her wings were multi-coloured. She wears a horned headdress and holds the rod and ring of justice, symbols of her divinity.
From southern Iraq, 1800–1750 BC. H 49 cm

The Royal Game of Ur

This is one of the oldest surviving board games in the world. According to references in ancient documents, two players competed to race their pieces from one end of the board to the other. The game was played all over the ancient Near East for about 3000 years.
From Ur, southern Iraq, about 2600–2400 BC. L 30 cm

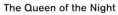

Middle East
Ancient Levant

The Raymond and Beverly Sackler Wing
Rooms 57–59
Upper floors, Level 3
8000–539 BC

The ancient Levant comprises modern Palestine, Israel, Jordan, Lebanon and western Syria. These rooms present the material culture of the region, from the Neolithic farmers of the 8th millennium BC to the fall of the Neo-Babylonian Empire in 539 BC, within the context of major historical events.

Objects on display illustrate the continuity of the Canaanite culture of the southern Levant throughout this period. They highlight the indigenous origins of both the Israelites and the Phoenicians.

Life for people in the Levant was defined by their dealings with their neighbours – firstly through trade and commerce, then through domination by the Egyptian, Hittite, Assyrian, Babylonian and Persian empires.

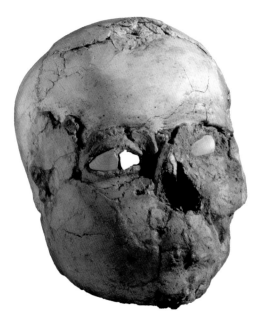

The Jericho Skull
The removal of the skull from the body and its separate burial was widely practised in the Levant during the early Neolithic period. As in this example, the lower jaw was often removed and then, carefully remodelled with plaster to build up the facial features. Similarly plastered skulls have been found at sites in Palestine, Syria and Jordan.
From Jericho, Israel, about 8400–7500 BC. H 20 cm

Statue of Idrimi

Idrimi was a king of Alalakh, a city-state in ancient Syria. The statue is inscribed in cuneiform with his biography. The text ends with curses on anyone who would destroy the statue, and blessings on those who honour it.

From Tell Atchana (ancient Alalakh), modern Turkey, 1600–1500 BC. H 1.04 m

Cosmetic box in a bronze bowl

This ivory fish-shaped cosmetic box was found inside a bronze bowl that had been strapped, using Egyptian linen, to the genitals of a body found in a grave at Tell es-Sa'idiyeh. This site controlled a shallow ford across the River Jordan. In the 13th century, it was under Egyptian control, during the final phase of Egypt's domination of the Levant.

From Tell es-Sa'idiyeh, Jordan, 1300–1200 BC. W 13 cm

Ivory plaque of a lioness eating a boy

This carved ivory panel was found at the Assyrian capital city of Nimrud in northern Mesopotamia. The carving is Phoenician in style, which suggests that it was made in one of the Phoenician centres along the Levantine coast and had come to the Assyrian capital as tribute or booty.

From the palace of Ashurnasirpal II, Nimrud, northern Iraq, 900–700 BC. H 10 cm

The Enlightenment was an age of reason and learning that flourished across Europe and America from about 1680 to 1820. This rich and diverse permanent exhibition uses thousands of objects to demonstrate how people in Britain understood the world during this period. It is housed in a magnificent room once known as the King's Library which was built to house the library of King George III.

Enlightened men and women believed that the key to unlocking the past and the mysteries of the universe lay in directly observing and studying the natural and the man-made world. Their passion for collecting objects, from fossils and flints to Greek vases and ancient scripts, was matched by their desire to impose order on them, to catalogue and to classify.

The gallery is divided into seven sections that explore seven major new disciplines of the age: the natural world, the birth of archaeology, art and civilisation, classifying the world, ancient scripts, religion and ritual, trade and discovery.

Merman
This 'merman' is made up of the dried parts of a monkey, with a fish tail. When collected it was said to have been 'caught' in Japan. This is the kind of curiosity that was found in early collections before the more encyclopaedic and reasoned approach to collecting evolved during the 1700s.
Possibly from Japan, AD 1700–1799. L 38 cm

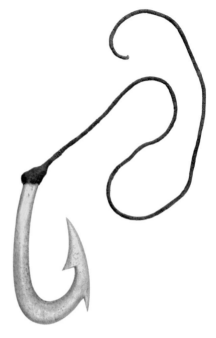

Shark hook
Captain James Cook (1728–1729) and his crew visited the Hawaiian Islands twice in 1778. This was the first time that Europeans had visited the islands and Cook was received with great respect, as he was thought to be an incarnation of the deity Lono, the god of agriculture and rain. Shark hooks were owned by high-ranking men, and shark fishing was a popular sport of the Hawaiian chiefs.
From Hawaii, probably AD 1700s. L 23 cm

The Piranesi Vase
The Italian architect and engraver Giovanni Battista Piranesi (1720–1778) engaged in the restoration and sale of ancient marbles. This ornamental vase combines expertly restored fragments of a figurative frieze discovered in the villa of the Roman emperor Hadrian (r. AD 117–138) with unrelated ancient and modern elements.
From Tivoli, Italy, AD 120–138, additions made in the AD 1700s. H 2.72 m

The Sloane Astrolabe
This astrolabe, that belonged to Sir Hans Sloane (1660–1753), formed part of the founding collection of the British Museum in 1753. Astrolabes are among the most sophisticated instruments made before the invention of the computer. They enable the user to determine the time in different hour systems at day and night, establish heights and angles and to facilitate the casting of horoscopes.
From England, about AD 1300. Diam. 46 cm

Founded in 1753, the British Museum opened its doors to visitors in 1759. The Museum tells the story of human cultural achievement through a collection of collections. This room celebrates some of the collectors who, in different ways, have shaped the Museum over four centuries, along with individuals and organisations who continue to shape its future.

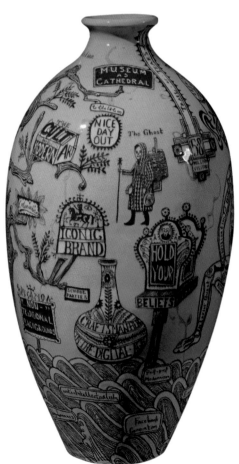

The Rosetta Vase (2011)
The Museum continues to actively collect objects from around the world. This vase was made by the British artist Grayson Perry (b. 1960) and shows the Museum as a place of pilgrimage where cultures and ideas meet. It was acquired by the Museum with funding from the British Museum Friends, whose support enables the Museum to fill historic gaps and to engage with living artists.
From London. H 78 cm

Figure of a hermit crab

This iron sculpture of a crab has articulated joints enabling it, when handled, to move as if it were alive. It demonstrates the incredible level of skill attained by Japanese metalworkers. The sculpture was part of the collection of Anne Hull Grundy (1926–1984), who formed the greatest post-war collection of 19th-century jewellery and also collected small and often elaborately decorated pieces from Japan.
From Japan, AD 1800s. L 25 cm

The Knucklebone Player

Charles Townley (1737–1805) amassed a substantial collection of Roman sculpture, it was described as 'the finest collection of antique statues, busts etc, in the world … collected with the utmost taste and judgement'. Townley was a Trustee of the Museum, which acquired his collection on his death. This marble sculpture shows a young girl playing a game with animal bones.
Roman, AD 1–199. H 63 cm

Figurine of a charcoal carrier

This figurine was collected by Henry Christy (1810–1865), who hoped that his collection would preserve world cultures and show how and why societies differ from each other. He collected this popular wax figure during his expedition to Mexico in 1856 where he observed local festivals and saw charcoal carriers like the one represented here.
From Mexico, AD 1800s. H 28 cm

Theme
The Waddesdon Bequest

Funded by The Rothschild Foundation
Room 2a
Ground floor, Level 0
AD 1500–1700

The Waddesdon Bequest is the collection of nearly 300 precious art objects from Renaissance Europe that was bequeathed to the British Museum by Baron Ferdinand Rothschild M.P., at his death in 1898.

The collection was accumulated by Baron Ferdinand and by his father, Baron Anselm, and was intended to rival those put together by rulers and princes from the Renaissance onwards. It is mainly made up of small-scale, rare and precious pieces of the highest quality that were intended to inspire a sense of curiosity and wonder.

Objects on display include masterpieces of goldsmiths' work, painted enamels, glass and ceramics, sculpture and small carvings in wood.

Huntsman automaton
This is a rare survival from German drinking parties of the early 1600s. It includes a mechanism that would have propelled it across a dining table as a trick wine cup. According to custom, the person the cup stopped in front of would have to drink all the wine from the hollow figure.
From Nuremberg, Germany, AD 1617–1620. H 31 cm

The Lyte Jewel

The 'jewel' was given by King James I (r. 1603–1625) to Thomas Lyte (1568–1638) in appreciation of his gift of an illuminated pedigree, which traced the king's ancestry back to the mythical founder of Britain.

From London, England, AD 1610–1611. H 6 cm

The Holy Thorn Reliquary

This reliquary was made to house a relic of the Crown of Thorns, the wreath of thorns placed on the head of Jesus Christ at his crucifixion. The thorn is displayed behind a crystal window and is identified by a Latin inscription.

From Paris, France, before AD 1397. H 30 cm

Rock crystal standing cup (*tazza*)

The marvellous translucency of rock crystal ensured that it was one of the most prized materials in European princely collections. Skilled techniques were required to carve, polish and engrave this very hard material.

From Italy, about AD 1550–1600. H 15 cm

This gallery explores how people everywhere deal with the tough realities of life and death. The displays explore different approaches to our shared challenges as human beings, focussing on how diverse cultures seek to maintain health and well-being.

Objects on display consider different approaches to averting illness, danger and trouble, and investigate people's reliance on relationships with each other, the animal kingdom, spiritual powers and the world around us.

In the centre of the gallery, a specially-commissioned artwork by Pharmacopoeia, entitled *Cradle to Grave*, looks at one approach to health and well-being, describing the medical histories of a typical man and woman in Britain today.

Door lintel
This wooden door lintel (*pare*) would have been placed over the entrance to a meeting house. The central figure has a double tongue with hands on hips and is flanked by small bird-like *manaia* figures. All figures have haliotis-shell eyes. The carvings help protect the host and visitors from spiritual danger.
Probably from Hawke's Bay, New Zealand, AD 1860s. W 94 cm

The Atomic Apocalypse (1983)
The celebration of the Christian festivals of All Saints and All Souls at the beginning of November have evolved in Mexico into a joyful and ironic commemoration of the dead, who experience a brief return to the pleasures of their former existence. This group of 132 papier mâché figures references actual events and areas of ongoing political conflict.
From Mexico City, Mexico.

Figure holding a fish
This carving commemorates a male ancestor, who would have been prayed to by his descendants for spiritual support and protection. The fish he holds shows his special powers for fishing. Figures such as this one were kept in shrines where the lives and achievements of local people are still remembered, but their descendants have now long prayed to the Christian god instead.
From Roviana, New Georgia Islands, western Solomon Islands, AD 1880s. H 1.26 m

Hoa Hakananai'a
This monumental carving made of basalt represents an ancestor figure from Rapa Nui (Easter Island) which is famous for its monolithic statues (*moai*) such as this. Hakananai'a means 'Stolen or Hidden Friend'. It's eyes were originally inlaid with red stone and coral and the figure itself painted with red and white designs. It was probably first displayed in the open air before being moved to a stone house at the ritual centre of Orongo.
From Orongo, Rapa Nui, Polynesia, about AD 1000. H 2.42 m

Theme
Clocks and watches

The Sir Harry and Lady Djanogly Gallery
Rooms 38–39
Upper floors, Level 3
AD 1300–present

Mechanical clocks were invented in Western Europe in the medieval period and were first used in cathedrals and churches. This gallery traces their development from the earliest examples to complex and highly decorative domestic clocks, marine chronometers, mass-market designs and modern precision time-keeping.

Often spectacular, clocks and watches tell the time but can also tell us about their owners. The first room shows early clocks, up to the crucial introduction of the pendulum in the 1650s. The second continues the story to the present day and also holds a magnificent selection of watches. Many of the clocks are working and can be heard ticking, striking and chiming.

Turret clock
By the late 1200s, clocks were being installed in cathedrals, abbeys and churches around Europe. The design of the turret clock changed little over the following few centuries – this example has similar characteristics to those made in the medieval period.
From England, around AD 1610.
H 76 cm

Rolling ball clock

The timekeeping of this clock is controlled by a rolling steel ball, which takes 30 seconds to zig-zag down the table and operate a lever, which causes the table to tilt and send the ball back. Over a year, the ball travels around 2500 miles (4000 km).

From London, England, AD 1805–1815. H 61 cm

Carillon clock

This clock is based on the cathedral clock in Strasbourg, France. Every hour it plays music written by Martin Luther. The weight-driven gilded-brass musical clock includes religious automata (figures that appear to move under their own power). It is located just outside the entrance to the two rooms.

From Strasbourg, France, AD 1589. H 1.57 m

The Mechanical Galleon

This *nef* or medieval galleon, would have been used to impress guests at a prince's banquet. Travelling down the table, playing music on a regal and drum, with sailors striking bells in the crows' nests, it would finally stop and fire its thirteen guns.

From Augsburg, South Germany, about AD 1585. H 104 cm

Theme
Money

The Citi Money Gallery
Room 68
Upper floors, Level 3
Prehistory–present

The history of money can be traced back over 4000 years. During this time, currency has taken many different forms, from coins to banknotes, shells to mobile phone payments. This gallery displays the history of money around the world. From the earliest evidence, to the latest developments in digital technology, money has been an important part of human societies. Looking at the history of money gives us a way to understand the history of the world.

Electrum *stater*
Cities and empires traded without using coins for over 2000 years. But when ancient Mediterranean kingdoms such as Lydia (in modern Turkey) began issuing pieces of electrum (a mixture of gold and silver) like this one, of a consistent weight and purity, the idea quickly caught on. This is one of the earliest coins in the world, and today the change in our pockets is based on the same inspirational idea that brought it into being.
From Lydia (modern Turkey),
about 650–600 BC. Diam. 10 mm

Suffragette-defaced penny
In the early 1900s this British penny was defaced to promote the suffragette cause. This bold criminal act was one of many that catapulted the movement for women's right to vote into the political limelight. The penny stands for all those who fought for this monumental change.
From United Kingdom, AD 1903. W 31 mm

Cowrie money

For thousands of years, cowrie shells were used as currency around the world, from China to Arabia and Africa. Their widespread use shows that people entrusted such objects a worth independent of their intrinsic value, enabling their daily trade.

Issued in West Africa, AD 1796.

Chinese Ming banknote

After seizing power from the Mongol rulers of China in 1368, the rulers of the Ming dynasty (1368–1644) tried to reinstate bronze coins. However, there was not enough metal available for this, and paper money, made of mulberry bark, was produced.

From China, AD 1375. H 34 cm

Theme
Prints and drawings

Room 90
Upper floors, Level 4
AD 1400–present

The British Museum holds the national collection of Western prints and drawings. It is one of the top three collections of its kind in the world. There are approximately 50,000 drawings and over 2 million prints dating from the beginning of the AD 1400s up to the present day.

The greatest strengths of the collection lie in the fields of Old Master prints and drawings from all schools, satires of the AD 1700–1800s, and British material of all periods. For conservation reasons, the prints and drawings are exhibited by means of a series of changing displays in Room 90. The public can also ask to see any object in the collection on demand via the Study Room, which is next to Room 90.

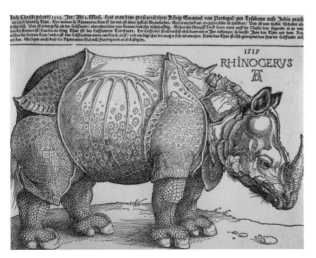

Rhinoceros by Albrecht Dürer (1471–1528)
This celebrated woodcut records the arrival in Lisbon of an Indian rhinoceros on 20 May 1515. It was sent as a diplomatic gift to King Manuel I of Portugal and was the first to be seen in Europe since the AD 200s. Dürer never actually saw the rhinoceros, and created this woodcut from descriptions, which explains the scales and hard patterned plates shown on the animal's body. This was the defining image of the rhinoceros for centuries.
From Germany, AD 1515.
H 21 x 30 cm

Epifania by Michelangelo Buonarroti (1475–1564)

This is one of only two surviving cartoons by Michelangelo. A cartoon is a final preparatory drawing on the same scale as the finished painting. This cartoon is recorded in Michelangelo's studio after his death. The subject remains mysterious, but the position of Christ between his mother's legs suggests that one of its themes was his miraculous incarnation. *From Rome, Italy, about AD 1550–1553. H 2.3 x 1.6 m*

Stately plump Buck Mulligan by Richard Hamilton (1922–2011)

This is one of more than 90 works in the collection related to an unrealised project by the British artist Richard Hamilton to illustrate James Joyce's modernist masterpiece *Ulysses* (1922). The drawing depicts the opening passage of the novel with Buck Mulligan in a dressing gown, the hovering ghost of the reproachful mother of his friend, Stephen Dedalus, hovering behind him. *From Britain, AD 1948. H 58 x 40 cm*

Dancers practising at the barre by Edgar Degas (1834–1917)

Degas began studying dancers in the 1870s and they became a principle motif in his work. He frequently visited the back stage and public areas of the Opéra building in Paris where the ballet was performed. However, he rarely made his studies there, preferring to work in his studio from memory or posed models. *From France, AD 1876– 1877. H 47 x 63 cm*

List of objects

▓▓ Africa

Figure (*nkisi*) of a dog 14
Throne of Weapons (2001) 15
Silk hanging 15
Man's Cloth (2001) 15
Sudanese slit drum 16
The Luzira Head 16
Benin ivory mask 16
The Ife Head 17
Asante state sword 17

▓▓ Americas

Zoomorphic stone pipe 20
Warrior shirt 21
Mask of the *Nulthamalth* 21
Clovis point 21
Huaxtec goddess
    sculpture 22
Double-headed serpent
    mosaic 23
Gold pendant figurine 23
Yaxchilán lintel 23

▓▓ Ancient Egypt

The Rosetta Stone 26
Statue of Ramesses II 27
Head of Amenhotep III 27
List of kings 27
Tomb-painting of a hunt
    in the marshes 28
Book of the Dead
    of Hunefer 29
Inner coffin of
    Hornedjitef 30
Blue-glazed *shabti*
    of Sety I 30
Mummy of a cat 31
Wooden stela of
    Nakhtefmut 31
Ivory label for King
    Den's sandals 32
Bone figure of a woman 33
Mudstone palette 33
Pottery group of cattle 33
Pottery beaker 34
Sphinx of King Taharqo 34
Wall-painting of the
    martyrdom of saints 35

▓▓ Ancient Greece and Rome

Marble figurine of a woman 38
Gold pendant from
    the Aigina treasure 39
Minoan bull and acrobat 39
Amphora depicting
    Achilles 40
The Sophilos Dinos 41
Gold coin of Croesus 41
Terracotta horse and
    horseman 41
Amphora depicting
    Herakles 43
Amphora depicting Dionysos
    and two satyrs 43
Lekythos depicting
    Odysseus 43
Tomb of King Kybernis 44
The Bassai Frieze 45
The Nereid Monument 47
Frieze from the Nereid
    Monument 47
Sculpture of Ilissos 48
Metope of a Centaur
    and Lapith 49
Sculpture of Iris 49
Sculpture of a horse's
    head 49
Marble block from the
    Temple of Athena Nike 50
Decorative relief 51
Marble head of Apollo 52
Horse from a chariot-
    group 52
Marble column drum 53
Statue of crouching
    Aphrodite 54
White-ground jug 55
Helmet of a Murmillo 55
The Portland Vase 56
Marble statue of the emperor
    Septimius Severus 57
Head of Augustus (The
    Meroë Head) 57
The Warren Cup 57
Gold brooch with lions 58
Woman with child 59
Silver *decadrachm*
    of Syracuse 60
Volute-krater 61
Bronze statuette of a warrior
    on horseback 61
Gold *phiale* 61
Lion's head spout 62
Defaced dedicatory
    inscription 63

▓▓ Asia

Figure of Shiva Nataraja 67
Bodhisattva Tara 67
Jar depicting a dragon 67
The Great Stūpa 68
Pair of *Buddhapada* 68
Jade headdress
    ornament 69
Moon jar 71
Guardian King of the North 71
*Samramansang Moon Jar
    #1* (2010–2013) 71
Celadon bowl 71
The Admonitions
    Scroll 72–73
Statue of Fudō Myō-ō 74
Samurai armour and
    helmet 75
Young woman mask
    for Nō drama 75
Kakiemon elephant 75

Vase with butterflies
and daylilies 76
Moon-shaped flask
with birds 77
The David Vases 77
Pear-shaped covered ewer 77

Europe
The Lewis Chessmen 80
Icon of the Triumph
of Orthodoxy 81
Parade shield 81
Citole 81
The Royal Gold Cup 81
Gold belt-buckle 82
The Franks Casket 83
The Sutton Hoo Helmet 83
The Lycurgus Cup 83
Bust of Oliver Cromwell
by Roubillac 84
Medal of Mary I by
Jacopo da Trezzo 85
The Medici Vase 85
Maiolica plate 85
The Pegasus Vase 86
Teapot designed by
Christopher Dresser 86
Russian revolutionary
plate 87
The Mildenhall Great
Dish 88
Hinton St Mary mosaic 89
Tomb of Classicianus 89
The emperor Hadrian 89
The Great Torc 90
Basse-Yutz Flagon 90
Gold cape 91
Red deer antler
headdress 91

Middle East
The Black Obelisk of
Shalmaneser III 94
Statue of a human-headed
winged lion 94
Panel of Ashurnasirpal II
with tribute bearers 95
Relief from the North-West
Palace of
Ashurnasirpal II 95
Stone panel from the
South-West Palace
of Sennacherib 96

Stone panel from the North
Palace of Ashurbanipal 97
Jade terrapin 98
The Blacas Ewer 99
Enamelled glass canteen 99
Footed basin 99
Peacock and stand 99
Griffin-headed armlet from the
Oxus Treasure 100
The Cyrus Cylinder 101
Relief of a winged
male sphinx 101
Silver plate 101
Tin-bronze altar with a
Sabaean dedication 102
Incense burner 102
Relief showing a
storm-god 103
Silver bull 103
Map of the World 104
The Flood Tablet 105
Lady Layard's Necklace 105
Brick panel showing a
roaring lion 105
The Standard of Ur 106
Ram in a Thicket 107
The Queen of the
Night 107
The Royal Game of Ur 107
The Jericho Skull 108
Statue of Idrimi 109
Cosmetic box in a
bronze bowl 109
Ivory plaque of a lioness
eating a boy 109

Enlightenment
Merman 110
Shark hook 111
The Piranesi Vase 111
The Sloane Astrolabe 111

Collecting the world
The Rosetta Vase (2011) 112
Figure of a hermit crab 113
The Knucklebone Player 113
Figurine of a charcoal
carrier 113

The Waddesdon
Bequest
Huntsman automaton 114
The Lyte Jewel 115
The Holy Thorn Reliquary 115
Rock crystal standing
cup (tazza) 115

Living and Dying
Door lintel 116
The Atomic Apocalypse
(1983) 117
Figure holding a fish 117
Hoa Hakananai'a 117

Clocks and watches
Turret clock 118
Rolling ball clock 119
Carillon clock 119
The Mechanical Galleon 119

Money
Electrum stater 120
Suffragette-defaced
penny 120
Cowrie money 121
Chinese Ming banknote 121

Prints and drawings
Rhinoceros by Albrecht
Dürer (1471–1528) 122
Stately plump Buck Mulligan
by Richard Hamilton
(1922–2011) 123
Epifania by Michelangelo
Buonarroti (1475–
1564) 123
Dancers practising at the
barre by Edgar Degas
(1834–1917) 123

Objects in grey feature
in *A History of the World in
100 Objects* a series by Neil
MacGregor, former Director
of the British Museum.